Leaves from our Tuscan Kitchen

or how to cook vegetables

The Kitchen
Poggio Gherardo
A.Marlow Marves
1895

Leaves from our Tuscan Kitchen

or how to cook vegetables

by Janet Ross
and Michael Waterfield

Atheneum   New York   1974

Originally published 1899
This edition copyright © 1973 by Michael Waterfield
Library of Congress catalog card number 73-91634
ISBN 0-689-10598-3
Printed by The Murray Printing Company,
Forge Village, Massachusetts
Bound by H. Wolff, New York
First American Edition

Contents

Frontispiece by A. H. Hallam Murray from the original edition
Line drawings in text by Michael Waterfield

Introductory Note

The first edition of this book was published in 1899 by J. M. Dent, and its last, the eleventh, in 1936. Nearly forty years have intervened and copies have become rare, but when found are among the treasured possessions in gourmets' households. There is today a growing interest in good cooking, a change from the end of last century when Janet Ross wrote in her Preface:

> Not so very long ago soup was an exception in English houses—almost a luxury. A dish of vegetables—as a dish and not an adjunct to meat—was a still greater rarity; and even now plain-boiled potatoes, peas, cabbages, etc., are the rule. . . .
>
> For years English friends have begged recipes for cooking vegetables in the Italian fashion, so I have written down many of the following from the dictation of our good Giuseppe Volpi, whose portrait by Mr. A. H. Hallam Murray, adorns this little book, and who has been known to our friends for over thirty years. . . .

Giuseppe was undoubtedly a very fine cook, as were his successors Agostino Sabattini and Carlo Guerrini, for many years a well-known chef in a London City bank. Maria Chiodetti, who still cooks for the family at the Castello della Brunella at Aulla, and worked for some time in the kitchen at Poggio Gherardo there acquiring the tradition of good cooking. Her vegetable dishes are specially appreciated by visitors who stay at the Castle. Janet Ross took great trouble in setting down the recipes from her chefs, to which she added others later. I found, however, that in editing the recipes and using most of them in my restaurant, there were some weights and measures which had to be corrected.

In editing these recipes I have omitted some elaborate dishes. Truffles in champagne, for example, which seems to have been dear to the Edwardians and delicacies which were remote in their aspic are now also remote in their appeal; but the form of the original book remains basically unchanged.

The vegetables are placed alphabetically for immediate reference, with mixed vegetables, salads, rice and spaghetti dishes taking their place at the end. Cross reference should not be necessary as each recipe is complete with its own sauce or manner of serving. All the recipes are for six people.

The lay-out of the recipes has been altered from Janet Ross's narrative form to one where ingredients and method are combined side by side, which should be easier to follow. Oven temperatures and a metric conversion table appear before the recipes.

I had always been interested in my great-great-aunt Janet, having heard about her adventurous life from my family, but it was not until I met the late Sir Harry Luke, who was himself a gourmet and the author of a fine cookery book, that I realised how well-known her book had become in its time. When it was decided to publish a new edition he was kind enough to say that he would like to write about the book and Janet Ross as a Foreword and, to my great pleasure, that is what he did.

The Wife of Bath,   MICHAEL WATERFIELD
Wye, Kent

Foreword

Leaves from our Tuscan Kitchen is the first cookery book I ever possessed; I made its acquaintance on one of the Tuscan holidays of my teenage youth at the same time as I made that of the authoress herself. In the sixty-six years that have elapsed since then I must have earned the gratitude of scores of my women friends through introducing them by means of this precious little volume—a blessing to him that gives no less than to her that takes—to the delights of the best Italian home cooking.

When Janet Ross's *Leaves* made their appearance in the antepenultimate year of Queen Victoria, Mrs. Beeton's monumental work of over a thousand pages still deservedly dominated the English kitchen, perhaps admitting from 1920 onwards in the houses of the more discerning eaters and drinkers the juxtaposition of Professor George Saintsbury's slender classic, *Notes on a Cellar-Book*, but of little else. The stream of the delightful cookery books— decorative, readable, practical—that nowadays fill shelf upon shelf of the gourmet's library, was then little more than a trickle, let alone coursing in full spate. Mrs. Ross's bantling was, so far as this country was concerned, something of a pioneer. Even in France, so infinitely more food-conscious than the British Isles, Brillat-Savarin, although sprung from an earlier century than Mrs. Beeton, was still the Frenchman's and Frenchwoman's unquestioned oracle on culinary taste and etiquette.

It says much for the intrinsic merit of Mrs. Ross's unassuming little book, now entering upon its seventh decade, that it should have achieved a viability in the literature of gastronomy hitherto attained only by the giants. But quite a number of contributory causes may explain this phenomenon. An obvious one is the perennial appeal of Italy to the peoples of the British Isles—an appeal promoted by the English humanists of the Renaissance; powerfully stimulated by the nobility and gentry of the eighteenth and early nineteenth centuries, who lumbered south in their coaches on the Grand Tour to return with acres of paintings and tons of statuary for the stocking of their

Palladian mansions; and since then maintained by the innumerable travellers of all ages and classes who delight to follow less pompously in their trail.

Another reason is the British people's growing interest in intelligent eating already referred to. A third, surely, is the fact that Janet Ross's recipes were those actually in use in her beloved Poggio Gherardo, that fascinating Trecento villa (in the Italian sense of 'villa') outside Florence with its echoes of Boccaccio and the telling of the tales of the Decameron. And then there is the personality of the authoress herself.

Janet Duff Gordon, afterwards Janet Ross, was born in 1842 and died in 1927; she was the daughter of the Lady Duff Gordon who wrote the celebrated *Letters from Egypt* and grand-daughter of John Austin, the jurist. Her youth was spent in a literary circle, and she is the Rose Jocelyn of Meredith's *Evan Harrington*. On her marriage to Henry Ross, a man more than twenty years her senior who had helped Henry Layard with his excavations at Nimrud, she and her husband settled in Tuscany, where she came to be regarded by some of her contemporaries as a somewhat formidable person. Even as a child she had been unusually strong-minded and she once refused a request to tie Tennyson's shoe-lace. She could certainly be alarming if roused, with her determined jaw, white hair and beetling black brows; her feud with Ouida has passed into the social history of the nineteenth-century Florence and, somewhat one-sidedly, into Ouida's *roman à clef, Friendship*. Yet she could be approachable by the young, as I, at least, found her to be.

For all too long, however, the *Leaves* have been out of print; and it is with a nice appropriateness that this new and long-awaited re-issue should be edited by Janet Ross's great-great-nephew, by profession a restaurateur. She, who produced at Poggio Gherardo not only books but a rather special vermouth, will appreciate that partnership from the Elysian fields.

HARRY LUKE

Preface to the original edition

The innate love of change in man is visible even in the kitchen. Not so very long ago soup was an exception in English houses—almost a luxury. A dish of vegetables—as a dish and not an adjunct to meat—was a still greater rarity; and even now plain-boiled potatoes, peas, cabbages, etc., are the rule. When we read of the dishes, fearfully and wonderfully made, in the old Italian *novelle*, we wonder whence the present Italians got their love of vegetables and maccheroni.

Sacchetti tells us that in the fourteenth century a baked goose, stuffed with garlic and quinces, was considered an exquisite dish; and when the gonfalonier of Florence gave a supper to a famous doctor, he put before him the stomach of a calf, boiled partridges, and pickled sardines. Gianfigliazzi's cook sent up a roasted crane to his master as a delicacy, says Boccaccio; and a dish of leeks cooked with spices appears as a special dish in the rules of the chapter of San Lorenzo when the canons messed together. Old Laschi, author of that delightful book *L'Osservatore Fiorentino*, moralises on the ancient fashion of cooking in his pleasant rather prosy way: 'It would not seem that the senses should be subjected to fashion; and yet such is the case. The perfumes, once so pleasing, musk, amber, and benzoin, now excite convulsions; sweet wines, such as Pisciancio, Verdea, Montalcino, and others mentioned by Redi in his dithyrambic, are now despised; and instead of the heavy dishes of olden times, light and elegant ones are in vogue. Whoever characterised man as a laughing animal ought rather to have called him a variable and inconstant one.'

The dinner which set all Siena laughing for days, given to a favourite of Pius II by a Sienese who substituted wild geese for peacocks, after cutting off their beaks and feet, and coloured his jelly with poisonous ingredients, forms the subject of one of Pulci's tales:—

'Meanwhile it was ordered that hands should be washed, and Messer Goro was seated at the head of the table, and then other courtiers who had accompanied him; and they ate many tarts of good almond paste as a beginning. Then was brought to Messer Goro the dish on which were the peacocks without beaks, and a fellow was told to carve them. He not being used to such office gave himself vast trouble to pluck them,* but did it with so little grace that he filled the room and all the table with feathers, and the eyes, the mouth, the nose, and the ears of Messer Goro, and of them all. They, perceiving that it was from want of knowledge, held their peace, and took a mouthful here and there of other dishes so as not to disturb the order of the feast. But they were always swallowing dry feathers. Falcons and hawks would have been convenient that evening. When this pest had been removed many other roasts were brought, but all most highly seasoned with cumin. Everything would however have been pardoned if at the last an error had not been committed, which out of sheer folly nearly cost Messer Goro and those with him their lives. Now you must know that the master of the house and his councillors, in order to do honour to his guest, had ordered a dish of jelly. They wanted, as is the fashion in Florence and elsewhere, to have the arms of the Pope and of Messer Goro with many ornaments on it; so they used orpiment, white and red lead, verdigris and other horrors, and set this before Messer Goro as a choice and new thing. And Messer Goro and his companions ate willingly of it to take the bitter taste of the cumin and the other strange dishes out of their mouths, thinking, as is the custom in every decent place, that they were all coloured with saffron, milk of sweet almonds, the juices of herbs, and such like. And in the night it was just touch and go that some of them did not stretch out their legs. Messer Goro especially suffered much anguish from both head and stomach. . . .'

A company of Lombard pastrycooks came to Tuscany in the sixteenth century, and introduced fine pastry into Florence. We find the first mention of it in Berni's *Orlando Innamorato*, where it is mentioned among the choice viands. Laschi says, 'the epoch of Charles V is the greatest of modern times, for the culture of the spirit induced the culture of the body'. But he does not mention vegetables or herbs at all. For them we must go back to the ancients. Bitterly did the Israelites, when wandering in the desert, regret 'the cucumbers

* Peacocks were skinned, not plucked, before cooking, and the skin with the feathers was put on to the roasted bird, and the tail opened out before placing the dish on the table. The 'fellow' ought to have cut the stitches and drawn off the skin, instead of plucking the feathers.

and the melons we did eat in Egypt'; though old Gerarde says, 'they yield to the body a cold and moist nourishment, and that very little, and the same not good'. Gerarde is however hard to please, for he says of egg-plants, under the old English name of Raging or Mad Apples, 'doubtless these apples have a mischievous qualitie, the use whereof is utterly to be forsaken'.

Fennel, dedicated to St. John, was believed to make the lean fat and to give the weak strength, while the root pounded with honey was considered a remedy against the bites of mad dogs. If lettuce be eaten after dinner it cures drunkenness; but Pope says:—

> If your wish be rest,
> Lettuce and cowslip wine, *probatum est.*

Sorrel is under the influence of Venus, and Gerarde declares that also 'the carrot serveth for love matters; and Orpheus, as Pliny writeth, said that the use hereof winneth love'. Flowers of rosemary, rue, sage, marjoram, fennel, and quince preserve youth; worn over the heart they give gaiety. Rosemary is an herb of the sun, while Venus first raised sweet marjoram, therefore young married couples are crowned with it in Greece. While

> He that eats sage in May
> Shall live for aye.

Sweet basil is often worn by the Italian maidens in their bosoms, as it is supposed to engender sympathy, and borage makes men merry and joyful.

JANET ROSS

Conversion tables

OVEN TEMPERATURES

Cool and very cool	200°F–300°F	$\frac{1}{4}$–2 regulo setting
Moderate	300°F–375°F	2–5 regulo setting
Moderate to hot	375°F–400°F	6 regulo setting
Hot	400°F–475°F	6–9 regulo setting

LIQUID MEASURES

1 Litre = $1\frac{3}{4}$ pints

2 pts approx. 1·15 litres

1 pt. approx. 0·57 litre

$\frac{1}{2}$ pt. approx. 0·28 litre

$\frac{1}{4}$ pt. approx. 0·14 litre

WEIGHTS

1 Kilo = 2 lb. 3 ozs.

1 oz. approx. 28 gr.

2 oz. approx. 56 gr.

3 oz. approx. 84 gr.

4 oz. approx. 112 gr.

5 oz. approx. 142 gr.

6 oz. approx. 170 gr.

8 oz. approx. 227 gr.

12 oz. approx. 240 gr.

1 lb. approx. 453 gr.

$1\frac{1}{2}$ lbs. approx. 686 gr.

2 lbs. approx. 906 gr.

Globe Artichokes/*Carciofi*

The globe artichoke is bred from the cardoon. In Italy there are two main types, the Moretti which are small and the Romani which are large and spiny.

They are eaten on the continent when half grown, the reason being that the leaves are more tender and the choke has not developed. In Italy the season is winter and spring. In England the most usual type grown is the larger spiny artichoke but far superior is the Gros Vert de Laon which is small and can be eaten whole.

The usual care must be taken in buying artichokes, that they are young and fresh and that they have not developed too much choke. They quickly lose their juice once they have been cut, which toughens the fibres in the leaves.

I

Carciofi Bolliti

Boiled artichokes; hot with Hollandaise sauce or cold with a special dressing

Cut off the stalks, pull off the outer leaves and trim the bases of

six large artichokes

Cut off, too, the top third of the artichoke which is inedible. Put them into plenty of

boiling salted water—

the base of the artichoke downwards. Cook for about twenty minutes or until the base is soft to the point of a small knife. If over-cooked they will lose their nutty flavour. Remove and drain well if they are to be served hot; or refresh in cold water and then drain if to be served cold. Once cooked they will not keep more than a day

If they are being served hot, prepare the following Hollandaise sauce while the artichokes are cooking:

Melt, but do not over-heat

6 oz. butter

Beat over hot water
together with
and

4 egg yolks
juice of ½ a lemon
a small pinch of basil

Beat the egg yolks and lemon until creamy and thickening. Then remove from the hot water and stir in the butter slowly and thoroughly. If it is not as thick as thick cream, return to the hot water and beat a while longer.

Serve the artichokes on a napkin
surrounding a pot of the sauce

If they are to be served cold, prepare
the following vinaigrette, taking
care to use the best olive oil

In a basin put

**a pinch of salt and pepper
a pinch of chopped
marjoram
and a teaspoon of French
mustard**

Stir in
and then

**2 tablespoons wine vinegar
6 tablespoons olive oil**

Mix well

Serve the artichokes on a bed of
lettuce surrounding a pot of the
sauce. If fresh marjoram is available,
put a small sprig in the top of each
artichoke.

2

Carciofi alla Francese

Small peeled artichokes boiled in water and oil and finished with lemon

Here is one of the finest ways of eating artichokes

Trim the bases and cut off almost half the tops

of twelve young small artichokes

Pull off about three layers of the leaves until only the light green tender ones are left. Cut them into quarters, putting them into a basin of cold water as they are prepared. Then put them into an open pan, barely covered with

boiling water with 6 tablespoons of good olive oil salt and twelve roughly crushed peppercorns

Boil until the water has evaporated and add the

juice of a lemon

Serve hot or cold with a sprinkling of chopped parsley.

3

Carciofi all'Italiana

Hot, boiled artichokes with a cold sauce Tartare

Trim the bases and the tops of	**six large artichokes**
Boil them in salted water for about twenty minutes or until the point of a knife sinks into the base. Drain and serve at once on a napkin with the following sauce:	
Chop very, very finely or liquidise	**2 anchovies** **a small onion or shallot** **3 sprigs of tarragon** **a tablespoon of capers**
Then add	**1 tablespoon wine vinegar**
And mix in	**2 egg yolks**
Finally blend in until it thickens, like a mayonnaise.	**6 tablespoons olive oil**

4

Carciofi alla panna

Small artichokes cooked in stock which is reduced, finished with cream and lemon juice

Trim the bases and cut off almost half the top of	**twelve young artichokes**
Pull off the outer leaves until only the tender light green ones are left. Put the artichokes into cold water as they are prepared	
Put them into an open pan, barely cover them with stock, with a little salt and pepper and boil fast until the stock has all but gone. Shake in	**¼ pint of cream**
Let it bubble and thicken a moment on the stove. Remove the pan from the stove and stir in	**the juice of a lemon**
Serve in little pots with chopped parsley.	

5

Carciofi fritti

Small artichokes, dipped in light batter and deep fried, served with lemon or tomato and garlic sauce

---

Trim the bases and cut off one third of the tops of

twelve young artichokes

Pull off the outer leaves and cut across into about four slices, putting them into a basin of cold water as you do them

Make the following batter:

Form a well, add

and

2 tablespoons (heaped) flour
1 egg yolk
1 tablespoon olive oil
pepper and salt

Mix and start stirring in the flour, adding about

½ cup water

Until the batter is like thick cream

Let it rest while you beat up the

white of one egg

Fold this into the batter
Heat two or three inches of oil in a deep pan until it begins to smoke. Dip the pieces of artichoke into the batter, drain for a moment and fry in the oil until golden

Serve with quarters of lemon or the following sauce:

Grate
into a pan with
add

½ an onion
2 tablespoons olive oil
a good pinch chopped basil
parsley
1 crushed clove of garlic

and

Stew for a few minutes then stir in

twelve sliced tomatoes

or a tin of tomatoes, season with

salt and pepper

and boil until creamy.

6

Carciofi farciti

Small artichokes boiled, stuffed with ham, chicken and cream, sprinkled with cheese and baked or grilled

Trim the bases and cut off one third of the tops of

twelve young artichokes

Boil in salted water for ten minutes, drain and remove the outside leaves until only the light green ones are left. Make a well in the centre of each one and liberally fill with the following mixture:

4 oz. ham and the pickings of a chicken (or about the same quantity as of minced ham)

Stir in

2 tablespoons cream
chopped parsley
salt, pepper and nutmeg

Put the artichokes into a well-buttered oven-proof dish, sprinkle with grated Parmesan and bake in a very hot oven or under the grill for 10–15 minutes. Serve at once.

7

Carciofi alla Barigoule

Large artichokes braised with pork, mushrooms and white wine

Trim the bases and cut off half the tops of

6 large artichokes

Boil for ten minutes, refresh in cold water and drain again. Remove the choke and fill with the following stuffing

2 oz. minced pork
1 oz. minced bacon
1 small onion, chopped

Stew these in a pan without colour, add

a little olive oil
8 oz. chopped mushrooms
salt and pepper

Cook for five minutes, stirring from time to time

Tie a rasher of bacon round each artichoke with string, put in an oven-proof dish with oil, fry lightly. Add a glass of white wine, the same of stock, cover and braise for just under an hour in a moderate oven. Remove the string and serve with the juices.

Asparagus/*Asparagi*

Of the many varieties grown in Italy, the commonest is the purple Genoa asparagus, in season from February through March into April.

It is a vegetable that should be simply served, but not one that is simple to cook. Having a woody stem and tender tip, it is easy to under- or over-cook it. Nor are the tinned asparagus recommended as an easy way out; being necessarily soaked in liquid for some time, they have little texture or flavour. (The best I have found to be the large white Argenteuils.)

Freshness is always important, not least with asparagus whose stems become woodier the longer they have been picked. The white stalks can be used for a soup.

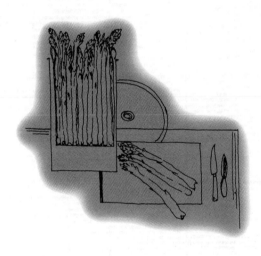

I

Asparagi

Asparagus; cold with vinaigrette; hot with Sauce Beurre Fondu or Sauce Mousseline

To be generous, allow one pound of asparagus for each person. Peel the lower white part with a potato peeler. Trim the bases and tie into loose bundles. Stand them upright in a deep pan and pour over boiling water, leaving the tips uncovered. Salt well and cover. Boil for twenty minutes and drain; lay on a dish and serve hot or refresh carefully in cold water and drain again, if they are to be served cold.

Sauce Vinaigrette
(enough for six people)
In a bowl, put

a pinch of salt and pepper
a pinch of sugar
grated nutmeg
the juice of $1\frac{1}{2}$ lemons
6 tablespoons good olive oil

Mix thoroughly together and serve with the cold asparagus

Beurre Fondu
In a small frying pan, put

6 oz. salted butter
a pinch of ground pepper
1 tablespoon cream

Heat, shaking the pan until the butter and cream emulsifies. Serve at once with the asparagus

Sauce Mousseline
Melt, but do not over-heat

6 oz. butter

Beat over hot water

4 egg yolks
juice of ½ a lemon
1 egg white
salt and pepper

Beat well until fluffy and thickening.
Remove the pan from the water and
stir in the butter slowly and
thoroughly. Return to the pan, still
beating until it is almost setting.
Remove from the fire and fold in

a heaped tablespoon of
whipped cream

Serve in a bowl with the hot
asparagus.

2

Asparagi alla Wilhelmina

Asparagus with a slightly piquant butter sauce

Peel the white part of five or six pounds of asparagus. Tie loosely into bundles and trim the bases. Put into a deep pan and pour boiling water in up to the tips. Salt well and boil for twenty minutes. Drain and arrange in a long dish.

Meanwhile prepare the following sauce:

Melt in a frying pan
4 oz. butter

Mix in
1 level tablespoon flour

Cook for a minute then, stir in
½ pint chicken broth
2 bay leaves
chopped parsley
juice of ½ an onion
salt and pepper

Bring to the boil and simmer for five minutes. Take the pan from the stove and whisk in
3 egg yolks
juice of ½ a lemon

Serve over the asparagus.

3

Asparagi alla Parmigiana

Asparagus with a butter and grated Parmesan sauce, finished under the grill

Cut off the green tips from four pounds of asparagus. Put into boiling salted water and cook for ten to fifteen minutes. Place in a dish and pour over them the following sauce:

Put into a frying pan

4 oz. butter
2 oz. grated Parmesan
2 tablespoons strong stock
ground pepper and nutmeg

Stir until the sauce bubbles. Remove from the stove and add

2 beaten egg yolks

Sprinkle with more grated Parmesan and colour quickly under the grill.

4

Asparagi alla crema

Asparagus with butter, cream and roast split almonds

Cut the white stalks off five pounds asparagus and boil the green tips in boiling salted water for ten to fifteen minutes. (Reserve the white stalks for soup.)

Drain carefully, put into a shallow dish and pour over them the following sauce:

Into a frying-pan put
and

4 oz. butter
2 tablespoons cream

Stir until mixture bubbles, add

juice of $\frac{1}{2}$ a lemon
ground pepper
3 oz. roast split almonds

5

Asparagi all'Italiana

Asparagus tips with coddled eggs and cream

Cut off the green tips of three pounds of asparagus (reserve the white stalks for soup). Boil in salted water for ten to fifteen minutes and drain carefully. Arrange the asparagus tips in ramekins

Break

2 eggs over them

Season with
and

salt and pepper
chopped chives (if available)

Pour over

a tablespoon cream

Pour a little hot water into the bottom of a roasting tray, put in the egg-dishes, cover with another tray and bake in a hot oven for about five minutes until the eggs are set. They can also be cooked in a pan with water over a gentle flame on top of the stove.

6

Asparagi ai gamberi	Asparagus with prawns and lemon mayonnaise

Cut the green tips off four pounds of asparagus. Boil in salted water for ten to fifteen minutes and drain carefully. Arrange flat on a dish

Pour over a	squeeze of lemon 2 tablespoons of oil salt, pepper and nutmeg

Allow to cool

Peel two pounds of large prawns and prepare the following sauce mayonnaise:

Put in a bowl	3 egg yolks salt and pepper grated rind $\frac{1}{2}$ a lemon
Stir and mix in slowly	$\frac{1}{2}$ pint olive oil
Then add	the juice of the whole lemon

Put the sauce in a pot, in the middle of a large dish, arrange the prawns round the pot and the asparagus round the prawns.

Beetroot/*Barbabietole*

How to boil beetroot

The smaller the beetroot, the sweeter and juicier they are. Wash them, taking care not to break the skin which will let the juice out in the cooking.

Put them in a pan in cold water and bring to the boil. For small ones, boil for an hour; larger ones for two hours.

Place them in cold water for five minutes and then rub off the skin. Use as required.

I

Barbabietole alla panna   Beetroot in cream

Boil twelve small white or red
beetroot. Cut into dice and pour over
the following sauce:

Melt in a saucepan	½ oz. butter
add	½ oz. flour

Cook for a few minutes

Then stir in   ½ pint single cream
                                     salt and pepper
                                     chopped chives or spring
                                     onions

Bring to the boil, stirring all the time,
and cook gently for a few minutes.

2

Barbabietole alla Lionese | **Beetroot baked with onions and milk**

Slice ten small boiled beetroot into a basin

Slice	**2 onions**
and cook them in	**2 oz. butter**
add	**½ oz. flour**
	½ pint milk
	salt, sugar and pepper

Bring the sauce to the boil, stirring. Mix in the basin with the beetroot and lay in an oven-dish. Pour a little cream over and bake in a hot oven.

3

Beetroot Salad

Slice twelve small cooked beetroot onto a dish. Sprinkle with tarragon vinegar, salt and coarsely ground pepper

Leave for a few hours and when serving, add olive oil or cream.

4
Barbabietole alla Parmigiana

Small beetroots, baked whole with cream and Parmesan cheese

Peel eighteen very small cooked beetroot and put them into a buttered oven-dish

Over them sprinkle

salt and pepper
½ pint single cream
chopped chives
2 oz. grated Parmesan
a few small knobs of butter

Bake in a hot oven and serve, perhaps, with hot tongue.

Broad Beans/*Fave*

Beans and peas must be eaten young, for with age the sugar turns to starch and the skin toughens. Broad beans are best eaten when they are no bigger than a finger nail and the pod, which is usually no longer than four inches at this stage, can be cut and eaten as well. (See *alla Turca*.)

All the following recipes use the cooking liquid as part of the sauce; this preserves more of the flavour and nutriment. If the vegetable is found to be cooked before enough of the liquid has evaporated, drain the vegetable into another pan, boil the liquid fiercely and finish as the recipe requires.

I

Fave al burro   **Broad beans cooked with ham**

Shell three pounds young broad
beans. Put them in a saucepan with   **a thick slice of ham**
                                       a stick of celery
                                       parsley
                                       3 cloves
                                       twelve peppercorns
                                       pinch of salt and a bayleaf

Just cover with boiling water and boil
fiercely for ten to fifteen minutes
until the beans are cooked and the
liquid has almost evaporated

Remove the celery and other
seasonings, chop up the ham and
return it to the beans and stir in   **2 oz. butter**

2
Fave alla Turca

Take three pounds of young beans
no more than four inches long.

Cut each pod into three, putting
them into cold water as you cut them

Boil in salted water for ten to fifteen
minutes, drain and mix in   **2 oz. butter, salt and pepper.**

3
Fave al vino

Shell	**3 lb. young broad beans**
Put in a pan and	**1 oz. butter** **½ an onion finely chopped**
When cooked stir in	**1 oz. flour**
Then add the beans, and	**a sprig of chopped marjoram** **salt and pepper** **1 teaspoon sugar** **¼ pint cheap white wine**

Just cover with stock and boil fiercely
until cooked.

4

Fave alla Romana

Shell three pounds of broad beans

Stew	1 chopped onion
in	2 tablespoons olive oil
Add	a large sprig chopped sage
and	1 dessertspoon tomato purée

Just cover with boiling water and boil
fiercely until cooked and the juice
has reduced. Serve hot or cold.

Broccoli spears

The season for good broccoli spears in England (early Spring) is short. They are picked when they are the size of a small cauliflower, fist size, with tightly bunched heads. They can be cooked whole when very small, or split into smaller heads with a small knife, prior to cooking.

They should be eaten simply, like asparagus.

I

Broccoli al burro

Take off most of the leaves and some of the stalk from four pounds of broccoli spears. Put them into plenty of boiling salted water and cook for about twenty minutes, taking care not to break the heads. Drain carefully and put into a serving dish

Pour over
sprinkle with

4 oz. butter
salt and rough ground
pepper

2
Broccoli alla Parmigiana

Prepare and cook four pounds of
broccoli in boiling salted water for
about twenty minutes. Drain them
carefully and lay them in an oven
dish. Pour over the following sauce:

In a saucepan, put	½ oz. butter
Heat and add	½ oz. flour
Cook for a few minutes, then add	½ pint milk salt, pepper and nutmeg
Bring to the boil, stirring well, then add	4 oz. grated Parmesan

Cook for a few minutes. Pour the
sauce over the broccoli. Sprinkle with
more grated cheese and bake in a hot
oven.

3
Broccoli all'Olandese

Prepare and cook four pounds of
broccoli spears for twenty minutes,
drain carefully and place on a
serving dish

Meanwhile prepare the following
sauce:

Melt, but do not over-heat	**6 oz. butter**
Beat over hot water	**4 egg yolks**
Together with	**juice of half a lemon** **a small pinch cayenne**

Beat the eggs until creamy and
thickening, remove from the hot
water and stir in the butter slowly
and thoroughly. Serve with
the broccoli.

Brussels sprouts/*Cavolini di Brusselle*

I
Cavolini di Brusselle al limone

Wash two pounds of very small
brussels sprouts and cut off the
outside leaves. Boil in plenty of
boiling salted water for ten minutes
until cooked through. Drain and toss
in a pan with

the juice of a lemon
2 oz. butter
salt and a good sprinkling of
coarse ground pepper.

2
Cavolini di Brusselle alla Milanese

Prepare two pounds of very small
brussels sprouts and cook them in
plenty of boiling salted water for
about ten minutes. Drain them well

Heat
and
in a frying pan

1 oz. butter
2 tablespoons olive oil

Add the sprouts and fry over a
rather fierce heat, tossing frequently.
When they are beginning to brown,
add

1 oz. breadcrumbs
1 oz. grated Parmesan

Continue to cook, taking care that
the sprouts do not break up. Serve
at once.

Cabbage/*Cavolo*

Cabbage is, perhaps, the most abused of all vegetables. If it is overcooked, it is quite useless for taste and food value. My publisher, Jock Murray, maintains that drinking cabbage water is excellent for general health and particularly for rheumatism. Cabbage, at any rate, deserves proper attention. Its cooking time will vary according to the type of cabbage, how fresh it is and how much stalk the leaves have. The general rule is to cook cabbage in plenty of boiling water, so that the water reboils quickly once the cabbage is added; alternatively it can be cooked (more usually the white or red cabbage) without any water at all.

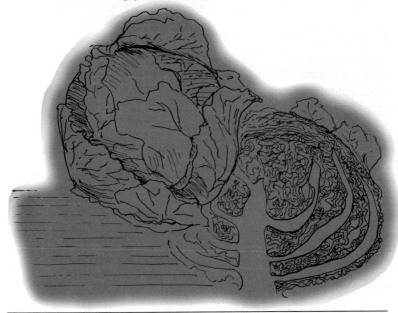

I

Cavolo al burro

Cut two large cabbages into six segments each, and cut off most of the stalk. Wash in cold water. Throw into boiling water with salt for ten to fifteen minutes, according to the type of cabbage and how stalky the leaves are. Drain, at once, and mix in a pan with melted butter, salt and pepper.

2

Cavolo alla panna

Cut one large white cabbage into four
and remove the stalks. Shred the
leaves across, not too finely. Wash in
cold water. Put into a pan of boiling
salted water for ten minutes, drain
well. Return it to the pan and add

½ pint thin cream
salt, ground pepper and
nutmeg
1 dessertspoon grated
horseradish

Cover the pan with a lid and finish
cooking gently, stirring the cabbage
from time to time. If the cabbage has
made more juice, remove the lid,
when nearly cooked and boil fiercely
to reduce.

3
Cavolo al forno

Cut one large white cabbage (or
Savoy) into six segments and cut off
most of the stalk. Wash in cold
water. Blanch in boiling salted water
for ten minutes, drain and refresh
under cold water. Drain well

Butter a shallow oven dish, arrange
the segments of cabbage in it and add

salt and ground pepper
½ pint stock
4 oz. butter in nuts

The stock should cover about a third
of the cabbage. Cover with
greaseproof paper and braise in a
fairly hot oven for about half an
hour, until cooked. Salt pork, ham,
sausages or garlic sausage added
before the cabbage goes in the oven,
makes a meal in itself.

4
Cavolo fritto

Cut one large white cabbage into
four and remove the stalk. Shred the
leaves across, not too finely. Blanch
in boiling salted water for five
minutes, drain well. Return to the
pan with

4 oz. butter
salt and cayenne
4 crushed juniper berries
2 tablespoons vinegar

Toss over a gentle fire until cooked.

5
Cavolo stufato

Prepare and blanch a white cabbage
as in the last recipe. Drain it.
Meanwhile cook

in

add

1 chopped onion
4 tablespoons olive oil
8 chopped tomatoes (or a
tin)
salt and pepper
pinch of mixed herbs

Add the cabbage to the sauce, cover
with a lid and finish cooking.

6
Cavolo alla Fiamminga

Cut two small red cabbages into four
and remove the stalk. Shred not too
finely and blanch in boiling salted
water for five minutes. Drain well
and return to the pan with

4 oz. butter
a grated onion
2 oz. chopped lean bacon
2 cloves
bay leaf, salt and pepper

Cook gently for about twenty
minutes until cooked and remove the
bay leaf and cloves.

7

Cavolo alla Tedesca

Cut two small red cabbages into four
and remove the stalk. Shred, not too
finely, and blanch in boiling salted
water for five minutes. Drain well
and return to the pan with

4 oz. butter
salt and pepper
sprinkling of caraway seeds
2 tablespoons wine vinegar
1 grated onion

Finish cooking over a gentle heat for
about twenty minutes.

8

Cavolo ripieno

Cabbage leaves stuffed with spinach and mushrooms

Cut off the main stalk of a large green
cabbage (preferably Savoy), and
remove the leaves. Blanch the leaves
in boiling salted water for five
minutes and drain well. Cut any thick
stalk from the leaves and fill with
the following:

½ lb. chopped cooked
spinach
¼ lb. chopped cooked
mushrooms
3 egg yolks
4 oz. fresh breadcrumbs
salt and pepper
2 oz. grated cheese

Wrap this mixture in the leaves and
braise in stock and butter in a
moderate oven for about half an
hour.

Capsicums (Peppers)/*Peperoni*

Peeling peppers is by no means easy, particularly in England where the peppers are not freshly picked. They can be plunged into boiling fat for a minute but the result is not always satisfactory. The skins, however, may be left on, providing the peppers are as firm and as fresh as possible. It is left to the discretion of the cook whether they be peeled or not.

I

Peperoni alla Spagnuola

Cut six peppers (red, green and yellow, if possible) in half and remove the seeds. Cut into thick strips

Heat, in a deep frying pan in it, fry

¼ pint olive oil
2 sliced onions
2 large cloves garlic (chopped)

and

the sliced peppers

When almost cooked, add

8 chopped tomatoes (or a tin)
salt and pepper

Finish cooking for another ten minutes, until the peppers are still slightly crisp. This can be eaten hot or cold.

2

Peperoni farciti   **Peppers filled with chicken,
                                         rice and thyme and braised**

Cut off the stalk end of six large
peppers and remove the seeds. Cook
in boiling salted water for ten
minutes; drain and fill with the
following risotto:

Fry, in olive oil   1 chopped onion
add   ½ lb. chopped cooked
                                         chicken
                                         4 oz. rice

Fry for a few minutes then add   ½ pint chicken stock
                                         chopped thyme
                                         salt and pepper

Cook for about 12 minutes until the
rice begins to swell, then fill the
peppers three-quarters full with rice
and stock

Put the peppers, open end up,
carefully in a dish, sprinkle with
olive oil and stock and bake in a hot
oven for twenty to thirty minutes.
Serve hot or cold.

3

Peperoni farciti

Peppers with pork, herbs and cheese

Cut six peppers in half and remove the seeds. Fill the halves with the following stuffing:

1 lb. pork sausage meat
2 eggs
salt, pepper and nutmeg
chopped chives
chopped marjoram

On each pepper place

a thick slice of Emmenthal cheese

Put them in an oven dish with pieces of butter and a little stock and bake in a moderate oven for about half an hour.

4

Peperoni fritti

Deep-fried slices of peppers with tomato and basil sauce

Cut six peppers in half and remove the seeds. Cut the peppers into half again lengthwise and dip them into this batter:

Make a well in
add

2 tablespoons flour
1 egg yolk
1 tablespoon olive oil

Mix and start stirring in the flour, adding

3 tablespoons water
a pinch of salt and pepper

until the batter is like thick cream

Deep fry the slices of pepper in this batter and serve with the following sauce:

Fry, in olive oil

1 chopped onion (small)
1 clove garlic (small)

when cooked add

8 chopped tomatoes (or a tin)
salt and pepper
1 teaspoon chopped basil

Cardoons/*Cardi*

Cardoons are the top stalks of thistle artichokes, delicious in flavour. They should be grown with the earth piled high so that the stalks remain white.

I
Cardi al burro

Peel three pounds of cardoons and cut them in two lengthwise, putting them into cold water as they are prepared, to keep them white. Cook in boiling salted water for ten to fifteen minutes, drain and toss in butter and a little more salt and pepper.

Cardi in umido

Peel three pounds of cardoons and cut them into two inch lengths. Blanch in salted water for five minutes. Drain, and dip in flour. Fry in olive oil until brown and cooked. Put into a serving dish, sprinkle with lemon juice and cheese.

Carrots/*Carote*

I

Carote all'aceto   **Carrots with vinegar**

Peel six large carrots, cut them into
four lengthways and remove some of
the hard centre core. Cut into inch
pieces, put into a shallow saucepan
and just cover with

cold water
2 bay leaves
3 tablespoons wine vinegar
½ minced onion
3 crushed juniper berries
a little salt and pepper

Bring to the boil and boil fiercely
until the liquid has almost gone and
the carrots are cooked. Sprinkle with
chopped parsley and serve hot or
cold.

2

Carote al vermouth   **Glazed carrots in vermouth**

Wash and peel six large carrots.
Quarter them lengthways, cut out the
hard centre and dice the remainder

Put the carrots into a thick pan with   **2 oz. butter**
add a pinch of   **salt and pepper and sugar**

Set the carrots in the butter for three
minutes

Then add   **1 wineglass cheap white vermouth**

Cover the pan and stew the carrots
rather gently, shaking the pan from
time to time. Add a little water if
the carrots get dry. When the
carrots are tender (about twenty-five
minutes) remove the lid and bubble
up the liquid until it thickens to a
syrup. Empty into a dish and sprinkle
with parsley. The syrupy effect of
this dish is not always so easy to
achieve due, I think to how much
moisture there is in the carrots. For
the final stage, when the carrots are
tender (if dry) sprinkle lightly with
sugar and add a little more vermouth
and toss over a good flame to
caramelise. This is a good dish with
pork and lamb.

3

Carote alla Parmigiana

Carrots and celery with Parmesan

Wash and peel six large carrots and three outside sticks of celery. Quarter the carrots lengthwise, cut out the hard centre and dice the remainder. Dice the celery and put both into a pan. Just cover with cold water, add chicken bouillon to season and bring to the boil. Simmer until tender. Strain the carrots and celery, keeping the cooking liquor. Put the carrots and celery into a dish and make a veloute sauce with the stock:

In a saucepan melt — 1 oz. butter
add and mix in — 1 oz. flour

Cook the roux and add the stock, bring to the boil and reduce until the sauce is the thickness of double cream

Then stir in — 1 oz. grated Parmesan
and — 1 oz. grated cheddar

Pour the sauce over the carrots and celery sprinkle with Parmesan cheese and bake in a hot oven for ten minutes (this can be prepared in advance and baked when required for fifteen to twenty minutes).

4
Carote alla casalinga

Top, tail and wash three pounds of
very young carrots. Put
them into a pan with cold water and
salt. Bring to the boil and half cook
for five minutes. Drain them and
return to the pan with

4 oz. butter
salt, pepper and sugar
pinch of rosemary

Cover with a lid and stew over a
gentle flame until cooked. Then add,
away from the stove,

3 tablespoons stock
juice of ½ a lemon
3 egg yolks, beaten

Shake the pan until the sauce
thickens, put into a dish and
sprinkle with chopped parsley.

5
Carote al forno

Trim two pounds of medium-sized
carrots, scrape them and put in a pan
of cold water to boil. Parboil for
ten minutes, drain and lay in a
buttered oven dish. Half-cover with
stock, sprinkle with salt, pepper,
pinch of thyme and small pieces of
butter

Braise in a rather hot oven, basting
from time to time, until cooked.

Cauliflower/*Cavolfiori*

I
Cavolfiori al burro

The best cauliflowers have small
tightly-packed, white heads. Trim
the outside leaves of three very
small, or two larger cauliflowers.
Cut a cross into the thick base of the
stem. Wash in cold water. Put into a
pan with plenty of cold water and
add salt and pepper. Bring to the
boil and cook carefully for twenty
or so minutes (longer for a very
large cauliflower). Drain with care
and put on a dish in a warm oven.
Prepare a butter sauce with:

**2 oz. butter
1 tablespoon wine vinegar or
lemon
salt and coarsely ground
pepper
chopped parsley**

Put the ingredients in a small pan,
let them bubble up, without
separating, and pour over the
cauliflower.

2

Cavolfiori alla Parmigiana

Trim two medium or three very
small cauliflowers and cut a cross in
the stem. Cover with plenty of salted
cold water and boil for about twenty
minutes. Drain with care, put on to
a dish and pour over the following
cheese sauce:

Heat	1 oz. butter
add	1 oz. flour
and cook	

Add	1 pint milk
stir, bring to the boil and cook for a few minutes	

Add and blend	salt and pepper
	grated nutmeg
	2 oz. grated cheese
	1 dessertspoon french mustard

Pour the sauce over the cauliflower,
sprinkle with more grated cheese and
brown in a very hot oven.

3
Cavolfiori fritti

Cut off the leaves of two medium cauliflowers and cut off the 'flowers' where they join the main core. Put into a pan of cold water and parboil for ten minutes. Dip each piece in beaten egg and breadcrumbs and fry in half butter, half oil. Sprinkle with grated cheese before serving.

4
Cavolfiori alla Piemontese

'Flowers' of cauliflowers cooked with onion, anchovy and marjoram

Remove the flowers from two medium-sized cauliflowers and parboil them for ten minutes. Drain them and return to the pan with

1 small grated onion
6 finely chopped anchovies
1 tablespoon vinegar
¼ pint olive oil
chopped marjoram

Cover with a lid

Cook for a few minutes and serve hot or cold.

Celery/*Sedano*

Choose fat heads of celery, not too long and stringy, nor brown from frost or being packed too tight. The very outside leaves and stalks can be used for soups and stocks.

I
Sedano fritto

Remove the outer stalks and cut off the leaves of three heads of celery. Cut into two-inch lengths and wash the pieces well in cold water. Parboil in salted water for fifteen minutes but it should still be crisp. Drain, dip in egg and breadcrumbs and fry in half butter, half oil.

2
Sedano all'Italiana

Celery, thyme and tomatoes

Remove the outer stalks of two large heads of celery and cut off the leaves. Cut into inch lengths and wash well

Into a deep frying-pan put

$\frac{1}{4}$ **pint olive oil**
1 chopped onion
the pieces of celery

Fry until the celery is golden and almost cooked, then add

$\frac{1}{2}$ **pint tomato juice**
salt and pepper
little chopped thyme

Cook for another few minutes and serve.

3

Sedano al forno

Celery braised with ham and bay leaves

Remove the outside stalks and cut off the green leaves of three celery heads. Trim the roots and cut them into four, lengthways. Parboil in salted water for ten minutes, drain and lay on a buttered oven dish with

6 oz. chopped ham or bacon
coarsely ground pepper
1 pint stock (half-way up celery)
3 bay leaves
small pieces of butter

Cook in a rather hot oven for twenty to thirty minutes.

4

Sedano alla Greca

Remove the outer stalks and cut off the leaves of three heads of celery. Cut into two-inch lengths and wash well in cold water. Parboil for ten minutes in salted water, drain and put into a deep frying pan with

½ pint stock
juice of a lemon
4 tablespoons olive oil
3 bay leaves
1 tablespoon coriander seeds
a little salt and pepper

Cook over a moderate fire until tender and the stock has reduced. Serve hot or cold.

Celeriac

I
Celeriac 'remoulade'

Peel a medium sized celeriac root
with a knife, cutting away any brown
patches. Slice it on a mandolin (or
finely with a sharp knife) and shred
into long matchsticks. Mix, at once,
with the following sauce:

In a bowl, put

2 egg yolks
1 tablespoon tarragon
vinegar
2 tablespoons french
mustard
salt and pepper

Gradually add

2 tablespoons olive oil
2 tablespoons thick cream.

Chicory/*Cicoria*

I

Cicoria brasata   Braised Chicory

Wash one and a half pounds of
chicory and if they are thick, split
them down the middle into two,
three or four. Lay them in a flat
baking dish with

2 oz. butter in nuts
1 cup stock or water and
chicken bouillon
salt and pepper to taste
juice of a ½ lemon
1 teaspoon sugar

Bring the liquid to the boil, cover
the pan and cook in a fairly hot oven
for ten minutes with the lid and a
further ten to fifteen minutes with
the lid off. Sprinkle with chopped
parsley and serve.

2

Cicoria con prosciutto   Chicory and Ham

6 very thin slices of ham
twelve pieces of cooked
chicory

Cut the slices of ham in two and
wrap each half round the chicory
laying them in a buttered dish. Pour
over a Sauce Mornay, sprinkle with
cheese and bake in a hot oven for
twenty minutes

Sauce Mornay
Melt   1 oz. butter
add and cook   1 oz. flour
add gradually $\frac{3}{4}$ pint milk or milk and
                                              single cream
add   2 oz. grated cheddar
                                              salt, pepper and nutmeg

Bring to the boil, and pour over the
chicory.

3

Tortino di cicoria   Chicory Tart

Line a six-inch flan dish with short
pastry. Roughly chop three pieces of
cooked chicory

Lay them in the flan

In a bowl mix

2 eggs
2 oz. grated cheddar
$\frac{1}{4}$ pint milk
$\frac{1}{4}$ pint single cream
pinch of salt, pepper and
nutmeg

Pour the mixture over the chicory in
the flan and bake in a moderate oven
for about thirty minutes until the
cheese and egg has set. Makes a good
simple meal with cold ham and a
green salad.

4

Insalata di cicoria   **Chicory Salad with hazelnut dressing**

Roughly chop three pieces of chicory
and put into a salad bowl

Toss with a dressing made as follows:

In a cup put

1 tablespoon crushed
hazelnuts
pinch of salt and pepper
pinch of sugar
1 juice of a lemon
4 oz. fluid cream

Mix the dressing thoroughly and
dress the chicory. Do not leave the
chicory too long undressed—it will
discolour. Sprinkle with chopped
parsley and surround the bowl with
washed watercress.

Courgettes/*Zucchini*

Courgettes are baby marrows, easily grown, and, I would think, becoming more popular than the large marrows. The season is the summer, the end of June through to September.

Courgettes survive several days after being picked because of their high water content; and for the same reason are preferably cooked without water.

The flowers (male and female), though without marked flavour, make excellent eating. They should be prepared within a few hours of picking to prevent them wilting.

I

Zucchini al burro

Courgettes cooked with a little water and butter in a covered pan

Wash two and a half pounds of *small* courgettes and trim off the stems

Put them in a thick saucepan with

**2 fluid oz. water
4 oz. butter
salt and ground pepper**

Cover with a lid and place on a low fire, tossing the pan until the courgettes are very nearly soft (*al dente*)

Serve in a hot dish with plenty of

**chopped parsley
and a squeeze of lemon**

2

Zucchini al pomodoro

Courgettes cooked with onion, garlic and tomatoes

Wash two and a half pounds of courgettes and trim off the stems. Cut them into inch lengths and put them in a deep frying pan with

**I medium sliced onion
2 cloves garlic chopped
4 tablespoons olive oil
a little salt and pepper**

Cover with a lid and stew for ten minutes, stirring from time to time. Remove the lid, turn up the heat and fry until slightly golden

Add

or
add more

**half a kilo tin of Italian
tomatoes or
I lb. peeled ripe tomatoes
salt and pepper**

Cook for a few moments longer only. Serve hot with roast meat or cold with fish salad.

3

Zucchini farciti

Courgettes stuffed with spinach and cream cheese and grilled

There are two methods for preparing the courgettes for this dish, depending on their size

If they are small, and therefore difficult to stuff, it is better to cook them in butter and a little water and then slit them ready for the stuffing. Allow four for each person as a beginning or six as a main course lunch dish

If they are larger (about six inches) trim off the stems and 'core' them carefully with an apple corer

In either case fill them with the following stuffing:

Soften in a bowl near the stove

3 demi-sel cheeses

Cook, for a few minutes

1 lb. prepared spinach or a packet of frozen leaf spinach

Refresh under cold water, squeeze dry and chop

Add

**1 whole egg
salt, pepper and nutmeg**

Mix all the above ingredients together and stuff the courgettes. (If the courgettes are cored, force the mixture in with a piping bag or small spoon)

The cooked courgettes have their cooking liquor poured over them, sprinkle them with grated Parmesan cheese and brown under the grill

The large courgettes, cored, stuffed and ready for cooking are laid in a dish with a little water, butter and seasoning and baked in a moderate oven. When cooked, sprinkle with grated Parmesan and finish under the grill.

4

Fiori di Zucchini ripieni al pilaf

A beginning dish of courgettes flowers filled with a saffron and cayenne pilaf and deep fried, served with tomato sauce

Allow two to three flowers per person

Fill them with the following pilaf:

Heat in a thick pan — **2 tablespoons olive oil**

Add — **a small pinch of crushed saffron**
4 oz. patna rice
a pinch of cayenne pepper
1 teaspoon paprika

Fry the ingredients without browning the rice then add — **½ pint boiling stock**
salt

Simmer until the rice is very nearly cooked and allow to cool

Meanwhile, prepare the following batter:

Put in a bowl — **2 tablespoons (heaped) flour**

Make a well, add — **1 egg**
1 tablespoon olive oil
pepper and salt

Mix together and start stirring in until the batter is a thickish cream — **3 tablespoons water**

Dip the stuffed flowers into the batter, drain and deep fry until golden

Serve the following sauce separately: **twelve sliced tomatoes**
(or a tin Italian tomatoes)

Put in a saucepan   **1 tablespoon olive oil**
½ grated onion
salt and a little sugar

Cook until creamy and pass through a
sieve.

5

Fiori di Zucchini ripieni di pollo	Courgette flowers stuffed with chicken

Allow two or three flowers per person and fill them with a tablespoonful of the following mixture:

Make a roux with	1½ oz. flour
	1½ oz. butter

Cook until sandy, add gradually	½ pint milk
	pepper and nutmeg
	a nut of chicken bouillon

Simmer for five minutes (the sauce should be thick) and then mix in	4 oz. finely chopped ham
	8 oz. finely chopped cooked chicken

Cover with greaseproof paper and allow the mixture to get cold

Dip the stuffed flowers in a batter made in the same way as in the previous recipe

Deep fry them, turning them once or twice and serve on a napkin with segments of lemon and watercress.

Cucumber/*Cetriolo*

I
Cetriolo alla Comasca

Cut some strips of peel from a
cucumber and slice the cucumber
very fine on a mandolin. Arrange
on a dish and sprinkle over

$\frac{1}{2}$ an onion grated (or very
finely chopped)
I tablespoon tarragon
vinegar
2 tablespoons good olive oil

Allow it to 'pickle' for fifteen minutes
before serving.

2
Cetriolo condito al miele

Cucumber with honey
dressing

Cut some strips from a cucumber, cut
the cucumber into inch
pieces and then into rather thin
wedges. Pour over the following
dressing:

I full teaspoon honey
salt and pepper
pinch chopped marjoram
2 tablespoons wine vinegar
4 tablespoons olive oil

3

Cetriolo al burro

Cucumber cooked with butter, chervil and lemon

Cut strips of peel from two cucumbers, cut the cucumbers into two inch pieces and then into thick wedges

Put them in a thick pan with

4 oz. butter
1 cup water
large pinch chervil

Cover with a lid and stew gently for fifteen minutes

Meanwhile, with a very sharp knife, cut the skin and pith from

2 lemons

Then cut out the segments from the dividing skin. Add the segments of the lemons to the cucumber, squeeze the skins over and shake the pan over a gentle heat

Add

2 oz. of butter in pieces

Remove from the stove and shake again

Serve with a meat dish that is cooked with fruit, such as lamb basted with honey or pork with apricots.

4

Cetriolo alla Spagnuola

Stuffed cucumbers, tied, and baked with onions, carrots and thyme

Cut strips of peel from two cucumbers. Cut the cucumbers into two lengthways

With a teaspoon, remove some of the seeds, the length of the cucumber. Fill with the following mixture and tie the two halves together

**8 oz. minced ham
8 oz. cooked minced chicken or meat
salt, pepper and nutmeg
pinch chopped thyme
1 egg**

In a long casserole fry in oil

**2 sliced onions
3 chopped carrots**

When almost cooked, remove and fry the cucumbers. Return the onions and carrots and add

**6 halved tomatoes
a small sprig thyme
6 peppercorns
a little salt**

Cover the casserole and bake in a moderate oven for half an hour, until the cucumbers are cooked. Remove the cucumbers. Pass the remainder through a sieve or Mouli. Remove the string from the cucumbers and pour the sauce over them.

5

Cetriolo alla Toscana

**Cucumber cooked with
butter, cream and nutmeg**

Cut strips of peel from two cucumbers
and cut into thick slices

Put them in a pan with

**4 oz. butter
I cup water
salt and pepper**

Cook over a rather gentle heat
without a lid and when nearly
cooked add

**I cup cream
½ nutmeg grated**

Shake the pan over the fire until the
cream thickens, empty into a dish
and sprinkle with paprika.

Egg-plant/*Melanzane*

Vegetables that are foreign to England were viewed with the utmost suspicion by the medieval herbalists. Egg-plants were called 'mad' or 'raging' apples and I imagine were scarce indeed. But they have always made a colourful impact in continental market displays and are obtainable in England, more or less, all the year round. Their colour is unique among vegetables and the capacity of the flesh to absorb oil and juices makes the egg-plant valuable in a vegetable stew or cooked with spices.

I

Melanzane fritte

Choose three large, firm egg-plants
of a smooth dark colour. Cut off the
peel and stalk and cut into thick
slices. Put them in a colander with a
sprinkling of salt and leave for half
an hour so that some of the bitter
juice may escape

Meanwhile, prepare the following
batter:

In a bowl put

2 heaped tablespoons flour

Make a well, add

1 egg
salt and pepper
1 tablespoon olive oil

Start stirring in the flour and
gradually add
until you have a thick, creamy
consistency

3 tablespoons water

Dip the pieces of egg-plant in this
and deep fry for about five minutes

Serve with a tomato sauce, made
simply with

twelve sliced tomatoes
2 crushed cloves of garlic
salt and pepper
bay leaf
1 tablespoon olive oil

Cook these until creamy and pass
through a sieve.

2

Melanzane alla griglia, Genovese   Grilled egg-plant with a basil and garlic sauce

Peel three large egg-plants and cut off the stalks. Cut into thick slices, diagonally, almost the length of the egg-plant. Put into a colander with a sprinkling of salt to draw out the bitter juices

Then season with

2 tablespoons flour
salt and coarsely ground pepper

Light the grill in advance, brush the grill tray with oil. Then dip the pieces of egg-plant in the flour and lay them on the grill, brush with oil. Grill on both sides, brushing with olive oil as they cook. Keep in a hot oven until they have all been grilled. Serve with the following *pesto* sauce. (*Pesto* can be bought in tins—use it sparingly)

Pound, in a mortar to a fine paste

3 cloves of garlic
2 sprigs of basil
4 chopped walnuts

Gradually work in

2 tablespoons olive oil.

3

Melanzane al forno

Egg-plant cooked with
tomato, garlic,
breadcrumbs and
Parmesan cheese

Peel three large egg-plants and cut off
their stalks. Slice obliquely and put
into a colander with a sprinkling of
salt until the bitter juice is drawn out

Meanwhile, peel and slice

twelve tomatoes

Crush over them
and make a mixture of

3 cloves garlic
2 oz. breadcrumbs
1 grated lemon rind
2 oz. grated Parmesan

Pour a little olive oil into the
bottom of a large, fairly shallow oven
dish, arrange layers of egg-plant and
tomato, add a little more olive oil,
press down and sprinkle with the
breadcrumbs and Parmesan

Bake in a rather hot oven for about
half an hour. Serve very hot (with,
perhaps, a grilled steak).

4

Insalata di Melanzane   A salad of sliced egg-plant
                              and tomatoes, cooked in
                              white wine

Peel three large eggplants and cut off
the stalks. Slice fairly thick and leave
in a colander with a sprinkling of
salt to draw out the juices

Meanwhile peel   **twelve tomatoes**
and slice them

Heat some olive oil in a frying pan
(until very hot) and fry the egg-plants
in it, turning rather quickly for they
will easily take colour. Keep those
that are cooked to one side, if there
are too many for one pan

Put them in the pan and pour over   **1 glass white wine**
add   **2 cloves crushed garlic**
a little   **chopped basil**

Let it bubble and reduce and then
empty the pan over the sliced
tomatoes and arrange on a dish when
cold.

Fennel/*Finocchio*

Bulb fennel is nowadays quite regularly imported to England, which is fortunate as it is a difficult plant to grow. The failure seems to be lack of fine weather at the moment when the plant is about to fill out, resulting in the fine feathery sprays of the herb fennel.

The bulb should be firm and white; discolouration and dryness of the outer sheaths indicate old age, which, alas, can happen with the time lapse in transport from abroad. The outer sheathes may, then, need peeling or removing. The green shoots and leaves are cut to the top of the bulb—these can be happily used as a flavouring for another dish. The flavour of fennel, cooked and uncooked varies in the same way as celery, and there are many who prefer the raw flavour. Fennel fritters, however, fried crisp and brown have a fine nutty taste and go very well with a grilled fish.

In Italy bulb fennel has many uses in a salad, very often a few slivers are mixed with the winter radish leaves or appear chopped on top of a tomato salad. In this way it is used for its crispness and as a secondary flavour. On its own it is best cut very thin and served with a pot of best oil and vinegar and seasoning, separate. This, as an accompaniment to a fine goat's cheese, both fennel and cheese being sprinkled with oil and pepper makes an excellent end to a meal.

I

Finocchi al burro   **Fennel with butter**

Trim the top shoots of four
medium-sized bulbs of fennel and
peel the outer sheathes with a potato
peeler (if white and young, this is not
necessary). Trim the base and cut the
fennel first in half and then each half
into three or four. Wash the
segments well and cook them in
boiling salted water (with a small
piece of lemon to keep the colour) for
about twenty minutes, until just
tender

Meanwhile melt in a casserole   **1 oz. butter**
and grate into it   **½ onion**

Strain the cooked fennel, drain well
and toss in the butter. Sprinkle with
grated Parmesan and serve in the
casserole. A good dish to go with
slices of veal with Marsala sauce.

2

Fritto di finocchi   **Fennel fritters with lemon**

Trim three or four bulbs of fennel
and cut them first in half and then in
thin segments, each piece held
together by the stalk

Heat the oil in the deep fryer and
make the following batter:

put the flour in a bowl and make a well	1 tablespoon (heaped) flour
add	1 egg white
and	1 tablespoon olive oil
stir in	½ cup water (tepid)
season with	salt and pepper

Dip the pieces of fennel individually
into the batter (the batter should coat
the fennel but not cling in quantity
to it nor contain too much water,
which will make the batter
disintegrate in the fat)

Fry the fennel until crisp and brown,
drain and place on a dish with a
paper napkin (keep in a warm oven
while the remainder are fried).
Serve with good-sized pieces of
lemon.

3
Finocchi al forno

Fried fennel with tomatoes and garlic with a crisp topping

Trim the tops and bases of four fennel bulbs. Halve the bulbs and cut into thin segments into a thick shallow gratin dish (or frying pan)

Heat
into the oil put
and

$\frac{1}{2}$ cup olive oil
1 onion thinly sliced
2 chopped cloves of garlic

Fry for a minute or two and add the fennel, continue frying stirring occasionally with a wooden spoon. When the fennel is beginning to brown and is almost cooked add

One twelve oz. tin of Italian peeled tomatoes, broken up, salt and ground pepper

Lower the heat and infuse for five minutes

This initial cooking can be done in advance

Sprinkle the following topping over the fennel in the gratin dish (or transfer into a gratin dish from the frying-pan)

$\frac{1}{2}$ cup breadcrumbs, roughly crushed
$\frac{1}{2}$ cup grated Parmesan
$\frac{1}{2}$ grated rind of lemon
1 chopped clove garlic

Bake in a hot oven until crisp.

French beans/*Fagiolini*

The best variety are the very small *mange-tout* beans, which are no more than two inches long. The stringless variety are more common and should not be more than three or four inches long and very green.

I

Fagiolini al burro or vinaigrette

Boil two pounds young french beans in plenty of salted water for ten to fifteen minutes (according to their size). Drain them, add 2 oz. butter, salt and pepper and toss

For serving cold, drain the beans once cooked, refresh quickly in cold water and drain again. Then mix with the following *Sauce Vinaigrette:*

Mix together	1 tablespoon white wine vinegar 3 tablespoons good olive oil salt, pepper and a pinch of sugar 2 chopped spring onions.

2

Fagiolini alla crema

Boil two pounds of young french beans in plenty of salted water for ten minutes until still slightly crisp. Drain and put into a saucepan with	a pinch of salt, pepper and sugar a sprinkling of chopped chives and parsley ¼ pint cream 2 egg yolks

Heat gently together, stirring, for five minutes but do not boil.

3
Fagiolini allo Zabaglione

**French beans with a
fluffy egg and butter
sauce**

Boil two pounds of young French
beans in plenty of salted water for
ten minutes until still slightly crisp.
Drain and put in a dish. Meanwhile
prepare the following sauce:

Put in a pan over hot water

3 egg yolks
1 tablespoon white wine
vinegar
1 teaspoon sugar
pinch of all spice

Beat until fluffy. Then add

2 tablespoons cream

Pour over the beans. Very good
with boiled ham.

4
Fagiolini in fricassea

**French beans with a little
garlic and basil**

Boil two pounds of young french
beans in plenty of salted water for
about ten minutes. Drain and serve
with the following:

In a frying pan, heat up

2 tablespoons olive oil
1 clove garlic, squeezed
1 teaspoon chopped basil
salt and pepper

Add the beans and toss in the sauce.
Serve very hot.

Haricot beans/*Fagioli*

I

Fagioli alla Romana   **Haricot beans with oil, anchovies and lemon**

Use the new season's dried beans, some commercial beans can be old to the point that they never soften. Soak one pound of haricot beans overnight in plenty of cold water. In the morning, drain and re-fill with cold water. Bring slowly to the boil without salt. Boil for about one and a half hours or until tender. seasoning with salt halfway through

Meanwhile finely slice   **3 onions**

Brown them in   **3 tablespoons olive oil**
then add   **6 chopped anchovies**
        salt, pepper and nutmeg
        some of the cooking liquor
        juice of a lemon
        chopped parsley

Mix with the beans and serve very hot.

2

Fagioli alla Fiorentina　　　　　Haricot beans with
chopped fresh herbs and
velouté sauce

Soak one pound of haricot beans in
plenty of cold water, over-night.
Drain, refill with cold water, and
bring slowly to the boil without salt.
Cook for about one and a half hours
until tender, seasoning halfway
through with salt. Meanwhile make
the following *Velouté* sauce:

Melt in a saucepan　　　　　　　$1\frac{1}{2}$ oz. butter
add　　　　　　　　　　　　　　$1\frac{1}{2}$ oz. flour

Cook for a few minutes

Then add　　　　　　　　　　　$1\frac{1}{2}$ pints chicken broth

Bring to the boil and cook for a few
minutes. Remove the pan from the
fire and add　　　　　　　　　　juice of a lemon
　　　　　　　　　　　　　　　3 egg yolks
　　　　　　　　　　　　　　　1 tablespoon mixed herbs

Mix the sauce with the drained beans
and serve with boiled chicken.

3

Fagioli alla polenta

**Purée of haricot beans
with butter and cream**

Soak one pound of haricot beans
in plenty of cold water, over-night.
Drain and re-fill with cold water.
Bring slowly to the boil without
salt and cook for about one and a
half hours until tender, adding salt
half-way through. Drain and pass
them through a sieve or Mouli.
Then add:

**4 oz. butter
¼ pint cream
salt, pepper and nutmeg**

Cover with lid or paper and put in
the oven for ten minutes.

4

Crocchette di fagioli

**Croquettes of haricot
beans**

Make a purée of haricot beans (as in
the last recipe) and put it in a
saucepan with

**1 egg
4 oz. butter
1 tablespoon white wine
vinegar
chopped balm mint
salt and pepper**

Mix well and allow to cool. Roll up
into balls or little sausages, dip them
in egg and breadcrumbs and fry
them in a frying pan in a little butter
and oil.

Jerusalem Artichokes/*Carciofi di Giudea*

Jerusalem artichokes are a tall leafy plant with very irregular bulbous roots. They are difficult to peel without wasting a good deal of the artichoke, it is thus easier to cook them first and peel them when they have cooled a little. Their flavour is slightly sweet and they become almost opaque when cooked.

I

Purée di carciofi di Giudea   **Purée of Jerusalem artichokes**

In a saucepan put

2 oz. butter
1 sliced onion
2 lb. washed chopped
artichokes
2 sticks celery
2 bay leaves
salt and pepper

Cover with a lid and stew gently on
on the stove for twenty minutes.
Pass through a Mouli. Mix with a
little thin cream to make a purée or
with about 1 pint milk to make a
soup.

2

Carciofi di Giudea alla Parmigiana

Peel two pounds of Jerusalem artichokes and boil them in salt water for about twenty minutes. Drain and cut into fairly thick slices

Meanwhile prepare a white sauce:

Make a roux with	$\frac{3}{4}$ oz. butter
	$\frac{3}{4}$ oz. flour
Heat in a saucepan	$\frac{1}{2}$ pint milk with
	$\frac{1}{2}$ peeled onion
	a pinch or small bunch of mixed herbs

Mix the milk into the roux and when it thickens and boils, reduce the heat and add

4 oz. grated cheese (Parmesan, Emmenthal or Cheddar)

Stir the cheese in, add a little cream if the sauce is too thick and mix into the sliced artichokes. Sprinkle with grated Parmesan cheese and bake in a hot oven for fifteen minutes.

Leeks/*Porri*

I
Porri alla casalinga

Cut off most of the green part and
the root of two and a half pounds of
leeks. Slit them, not all the way
through, from the root up and wash
thoroughly. Put into boiling salted
water for five minutes. Drain and
refresh in cold water

Smear a shallow baking dish with
dripping, arrange the leeks in it; add

**little pieces of dripping
a sprinkling of sugar
salt and crushed pepper
a pinch of mixed herbs**

Then barely cover with
and braise in a moderate oven for
thirty to forty minutes.

stock

2
Porri alla crema

Prepare six good-sized leeks and
wash them well (cut off most of the
green, the roots and slit them
half-way through). Blanch them in
boiling salted water for ten minutes
and drain them.

Cut each leek into four, length-ways,
and arrange them in the bottom of a
buttered, shallow oven-dish

Sprinkle with

and pour over

coarsely ground pepper-
corns
salt
½ pint cream (thin)

Bake in a moderate oven for twenty
minutes to half an hour. Sprinkle
with parsley.

3
Porri alla Greca

Prepare six good-sized leeks and
wash them well (cut off most of the
green, the roots and slit them
half-way through). Cut them into
four, lengthways, and put in a large
frying-pan or oven-dish with

½ cup olive oil
2 oz. coriander seeds
1 cup white wine
1 cup water
salt and pepper
3 bay leaves

Bring to the boil on top of the stove
and cook without a lid, stirring
carefully until the leeks are cooked
and the juice is reduced. Serve hot or
cold.

Lentils/*Lenticchie*

Lentils need not be soaked before being cooked but a few hours in cold water often helps, for the longer the lentils have been stored, the more dehydrated they can become.

I

Lenticchie alla corona

Lentils cooked with pork knuckles and anchovies

In a pan, put

1 lb. lentils
2 knuckles pork
2 onions sliced
1 carrot sliced
6 peppercorns
2 bay leaves
2 pints stock

Bring to the boil, skim and simmer gently until the pork and lentils are cooked (about one and a half hours). If the lentils have absorbed all the liquid, add more as they cook. Finally, mince or chop finely add a pinch of

6 anchovies
mixed herbs

Stir these into the lentils and serve very hot, having cut the knuckle meat from the bone.

2

Lenticchie alla Provenzale

Soak one pound of lentils in cold
water for a few hours. Put them in a
pan with

I onion
I carrot
salt

Cover well with
and bring to the boil. Simmer until
quite soft (one and a half to two hours).
Drain them and pass through a sieve
(or Mouli)

water

Reheat and add
and

2 oz. butter
4 oz. cream

Serve with hot boiled bacon or saddle
of hare.

3

Lenticchie alla Romagnola

Cook one pound of lentils with

twelve peeled tomatoes (or
I tin of tomatoes)
½ cup olive oil
salt and pepper
2 onions chopped very fine
2 chopped cloves garlic

Just cover with water and bring to
the boil. Simmer, stirring constantly
and adding water when the lentils
become too dry

Serve with roast lamb.

Lettuce/*Lattuga*

I

Lettuce Salads

Wash two lettuces using the tender leaves; leave in cold water until wanted and then shake dry. Here are three dressings which go well with lettuce—but these are only three out of many.

Lettuce Dressing 1

Chop, quite finely	**2 hard boiled egg yolks**
beat in	**1 tablespoon good olive oil**
add	**salt and pepper**
	1 teaspoon mustard
	2 tablespoons wine vinegar
	3 tablespoons olive oil

Stir well together and mix into the salad.

Lettuce Dressing 2

This is best with Cos lettuce

Mix together	**salt and pepper**
	good pinch sugar
	1 dessertspoon finely chopped capers
	2 tablespoons tarragon vinegar
	4 tablespoons good olive oil

Cut one good Cos lettuce across into three. Wash and shake dry

Put in a bowl with	**twelve or more Nasturtium flowers**

Mix in the dressing.

Wash and dry the lettuce

Mix together	**half a clove garlic finely crushed** **salt and coarsely pounded pepper**
Pour over the lettuce	**a dessertspoon chopped chives**
And mix	**2 tablespoons white wine vinegar** **4 tablespoons olive oil.**

2

Lattughe farcite

Wash six lettuces keeping them whole. Plunge them in boiling salted water until the water reboils. Drain, refresh under cold water and squeeze dry.

Carefully open out the lettuces and put a tablespoon, in each, of the following stuffing:

6 oz. minced cooked chicken or meat
2 oz. fresh breadcrumbs
2 oz. minced chicken livers
1 egg
salt, pepper and nutmeg
pinch of mixed herbs

Lay the lettuces in a buttered, shallow oven-dish (just large enough) and add

1 glass marsala
2 oz. butter in pieces

Cover with a lid and bake for twenty minutes in a moderate oven.

3
Fritto di Lattughe

Wash twelve small lettuces, keeping them whole. Plunge them in boiling, salted water until the water reboils. Drain, refresh under cold water and squeeze them dry

Then dip them in the following batter and deep fry, until the root is tender

Make a well with the flour, add the other ingredients and gradually mix in the flour, to a smooth cream

2 heaped tablespoons flour
1 tablespoon olive oil
1 egg yolk
2 tablespoons water
salt and pepper

Serve, perhaps, with roast chicken.

Mushrooms/*Funghi*

Here is a list of some of the mushrooms easily found in the Tuscan hills or bought in the markets. The cèpes (*porcini*) are the most sought after and are often sliced and dried for use during the year.

Pratajnoli   (Cultivated or field mushroom)
Porcini   (Boletus edulis)
Prugnuoli   (Agaricus Georgii)
Dormienti   (Hygrophorus marzuolus)
Ovoli   (Amanita caesarea)

I

Funghi alla crema	**Mushrooms and tarragon cream**

Stew, over a good fire with	2 lb. small mushrooms 2 sprigs chopped tarragon 4 oz. butter
When the liquid has evaporated add	salt and pepper
Colour the mushrooms slightly, then add—still with full fire—	½ pint thin cream

Let it bubble until it has thickened a little, serve into little individual dishes and sprinkle with chopped parsley.

2

Funghi alla casalinga	**Mushrooms in butter with anchovy, mint and lemon juice**

Fry, in a deep frying-pan	2 lb. mushrooms 4 oz. butter 1 tablespoon olive oil
After five minutes, add	salt and coarsely ground pepper 4 chopped anchovies 2 sprigs chopped mint
Mix together and then squeeze over	juice of 1½ lemons

Fry for a moment longer, sprinkle with parsley and serve.

3

| **Funghi alla Francese** | **Mushrooms marinated in oil and herbs, and fried** |

In a casserole, put | **2 lb. mushrooms**

Pickle them with | **salt and pepper**
2 bay leaves chopped
¼ pint good olive oil
small bunch fresh chopped
mixed herbs

for one hour

Then put the casserole over a fierce fire and cook the mushrooms for ten minutes. Serve with a slice of hot ham.

4

| **Funghi al pomodoro** | **Mushrooms cooked with garlic and tomatoes** |

In a thick frying-pan, fry in | **2 lb. mushrooms**
4 tablespoons olive oil

After five minutes add | **salt and pepper**
2 cloves chopped garlic
8 tomatoes peeled, pipped
and chopped

Cook a few minutes more and sprinkle with chopped parsley.

5

Funghi all'intingolo   **Mushrooms cooked with onions, parsley and white wine**

In a thick frying-pan, fry   2 lb. mushrooms
in   4 oz. butter
with   2 sliced onions

Cook for eight minutes, then add   1 glass white wine
                                     salt and pepper
                                     plenty of chopped parsley.

6

Funghi alla pagnotta

This is a good way of cooking cèpes or any edible funghi.

Cook the cèpes as in the previous recipe and meanwhile, cut the top off a small, round loaf, scoop out the bread and fill with the mushrooms. Replace the top slice.

Put the loaf in a roasting tray on a bed of slices of streaky bacon and bake in a hot oven for fifteen minutes, basting once or twice.

7

Insalata di funghi

Slice   1 lb. mushrooms
marinate them in   olive oil
                                     salt and pepper
                                     chopped parsley
                                     3 chopped anchovies
                                     juice of a lemon

Serve after half an hour.

Onions/*Cipolle*

I
Cipolle al forno

Choose six medium-sized onions, and
without peeling them, push a sprig
of fresh basil, marjoram or thyme
into the middle with the point of a
small knife. Wrap each one in foil
and bake in a moderate oven until
soft. Remove the foil and the outer
skin and serve with a little melted
butter over and a sprinkling of
parsley.

2
Cipolle farcite   Baked, stuffed onions

Bake six large onions in metal foil
and when soft remove the foil and
outer skin. Scoop out the centre of
the onions which are to be chopped
with the following ingredients:

4 oz. ham (or remains of
joint)
2 oz. breadcrumbs
1 oz. melted butter
2 tablespoons cream
salt, pepper and chopped
marjoram

Mix the stuffing well, fill the onions,
place in a baking dish and sprinkle
with grated Parmesan and little
pieces of butter. Bake for a further
fifteen minutes in a hot oven.

3
Cipolle fritte

Peel and slice into rings   **4 medium onions**

Separate them into a bowl,
sprinkle milk over and leave them for
half an hour.

Drain them well and dip them in
seasoned flour. Deep fry for three or
four minutes. Drain well and sprinkle
with salt and pepper.

4
Cipolle glassate   Glazed onions

Soak in cold water for a few
minutes   **$1\frac{1}{2}$ lb. small pickling onions**

Peel them and put them in a frying-
pan with   **2 oz. butter**

Toss them over a medium fire for
ten minutes then add   **$1\frac{1}{2}$ oz. sugar**
           salt and pepper

Continue cooking without a lid with   **$\frac{1}{2}$ glass port or sherry**
until the onions are cooked and   **1 glass of water**
the liquid syrupy.

Parsnips/*Pastinace*

I
Pastinace al burro

Peel six young parsnips into a basin
of cold water. Cut them in half and
then into long thin batons

Put them in a deep frying-pan with

**3 oz. butter
juice of a lemon
salt and pepper
1 cup water
or stock**

Bring to the boil and cook,
uncovered, until the liquid is reduced
and the parsnips are cooked (add
more liquid if the parsnips are not
quite cooked).

2

Pastinace al forno

Parboil six peeled parsnips for five
minutes. Cut them into batons and
put them in a frying pan with
dripping. Roast them in the oven
(they can be put in with a joint).
When the parsnips are cooked,
remove most of the fat and add a
tablespoon of flour and brown on
the fire. Add a cup of stock, bubble
for a few minutes. Sprinkle with
plenty of Parmesan and brown for
ten minutes in the oven.

3

Pastinace fritte

Cut six peeled parsnips into batons
and boil them in salted water until
tender. Drain them, sprinkle with
salt and pepper, then dip them in
melted butter, and then in a mixture
of half flour, half sugar

Heat two cups of dripping in a deep
frying pan, put in the parsnips until
they are browned on both sides.

Peas/*Piselli*

It is sad that small garden peas are nowadays very difficult to find in the shops. Usually it is the pale dry pods of the field peas, whose sweetness has become starchy, that are offered. Perhaps the good quality peas are all under contract to the big freezing companies. Home-grown peas, whether the sweet garden pea or the *petit pois* variety are always the best. Most of these recipes, however, can easily be adapted by using frozen *petit pois* and adding other ingredients while the peas are still frozen.

I
Piselli al burro

Put a two pint jugful of shelled peas in a
saucepan with

a cup of water
4 oz. butter
salt and pepper
dessertspoon sugar
and some parsley or mint

Place on a hot fire, when boiling
remove the lid and stir from time to
time until cooked. Remove the
parsley or mint.

2
Piselli all'antica

Cook the peas as in the previous
recipe using a lettuce instead of
parsley or mint. Remove the lettuce
when the peas are cooked and shake
in

4 oz. thick cream

3

Piselli alla Borghese

Shell enough peas to fill a two pint jug
and meanwhile cook gently
and

I finely chopped onion
2 chopped slices of ham
in 2 oz. butter

Add the peas, a bunch of herbs, salt
and pepper and

2 cups of good stock

Boil fiercely until cooked and the
liquid has reduced.

4

Piselli alla Francese

Put a two pint jugful of shelled peas
in a saucepan with

2 chopped lettuces
I chopped onion
stewed in butter
salt and pepper
2 cups good stock

Cook over a good heat, stirring from
time to time.

5

Piselli nel guscio   **Peas in their pods**

Remove the stalks from two pounds
of very young peas and cook them
in their pods in plenty of boiling
salted water for nearly half an hour,
drain and serve with melted butter.

6

Sformato di piselli   **Pease-pudding**

Boil two pints of large shelled peas in   1 pint strong stock
with   salt and pepper
and a   pinch of allspice

When cooked pass the peas through
a fine sieve and return to a low flame,
adding   2 oz. butter
                                          1 tablespoon flour
                                          3 yolks of eggs
                                          2 crushed macaroons

Heat through stirring well, remove
from the fire and cool slightly while
you beat   three egg whites

Fold them in and put the mixture in
a buttered soufflé dish. Cook in a
container of hot water in a moderate
oven for half an hour.

Polenta/Maize flour

Maize flour is not much used now, even in Italy, where Northerners are sometimes called *polentoni* by the Southerners. The most successful use for maize flour is in making bread when it would be mixed with wheat flour; two-thirds maize flour to one-third wheat flour. It is a bread that goes well with a meal, particularly a simple meal of salami and cheese.

I
Polenta alla Parmigiana

Stir, a little at a time, into

1 pint boiling salted water
1 lb. Indian cornflour

Boil until smooth, then turn out into an oiled tray, spreading out the mixture until it is half an inch thick

When cool cut it into inch pieces and pile in layers in a baking dish interspersed, liberally, with melted butter and grated Parmesan, finishing with butter and Parmesan. Bake in a medium oven for forty minutes.

2

Polenta con salcicce   **Polenta with garlic sausage or zampone**

Make the polenta as in the last recipe
and cool on a tray. While it is
cooking, boil some garlic sausage—or
the rich Italian *zampone*, for half an
hour

Skin and dice the sausage, mix it with
some tomato purée and a little stock.
Pile alternate layers of polenta and
sausage in a baking dish with grated
Parmesan and pieces of butter between
each layer. Sprinkle finally with
Parmesan and butter and bake in the
oven for half an hour

Serve very hot with a crisp salad
with a slightly sweetened dressing.

Potatoes/*Patate*

I

Patate alla Borghese

Potatoes with butter and lemon

Boil two pounds of potatoes in their skins (or two pounds of new potatoes scraped). Drain and peel them and cut in thick slices into a shallow oven-proof dish

Add

4 oz. butter
chopped parsley
salt and pepper

Simmer with a lid and add

the juice of 2 lemons

Serve hot.

2

Patate alla campagnuola

Sliced potatoes with nutmeg and cream

Boil two pounds of potatoes in their skins, drain, peel and slice them thin

Heat them in a thick frying pan with

4 oz. butter
salt and pepper
nutmeg

Colour slightly, add

$\frac{1}{4}$ pint cream

Shake thoroughly and serve hot.

3

Patate in casseruola

A ring of mashed potatoes with a centre of tomato pulp

Peel and chop
put in a pan with
and

8 good-sized ripe tomatoes
juice of $\frac{1}{2}$ an onion
2 tablespoons olive oil
salt and pepper

Cook slowly while you prepare the potatoes

Mix in a saucepan, over a low fire

1 lb. mashed potato
4 egg yolks
$\frac{1}{4}$ pint cream
2 oz. butter

Stir frequently until the potatoes form a paste then season with
and arrange in spoonfuls round a dish

salt and pepper

Pour the tomato into the centre of the ring and sprinkle with grated Parmesan.

4
Patate alla crema

Boil twelve potatoes in their skins.
Drain, peel and chop them

In a pan, put

4 oz. butter
½ onion chopped
chopped parsley
chopped mint
salt and pepper

Stew with a lid on until the onion is
cooked. Then remove the lid, mix
in the potatoes and a cup of single
cream

Shake well until the mixture boils.
Sprinkle with parsley and serve.

5
Crocchette di patate

Boil eight potatoes. Drain well and
leave the pan on the side of the stove
for a minute to dry out the potatoes

Put them through a sieve or Mouli
and put the purée in the saucepan
with:

**2 egg yolks
a little grated onion
juice of a lemon
chopped parsley
2 oz. butter
2 tablespoons of cream
a pinch of cinnamon and
grated nutmeg
salt and pepper**

Mix the purée with these ingredients
thoroughly with a wooden spoon on
a low fire until the mixture stiffens.
When cool, roll into little sausages
on a floured board. Egg and
breadcrumb and fry in hot fat until
golden.

6

Patate al forno

Bake six large potatoes. When
cooked, cut them in two and remove
the insides with a spoon. Mash the
scooped out potato with a fork and
add

4 oz. butter
½ pint hot milk
salt and pepper
6 crushed juniper berries

Mix well together and add the beaten   whites of 2 eggs

Fill the skins with the paste and fork
over the top

Cook in a hot oven until crisp and
golden.

7
Gnocchi di patate

Boil eight potatoes. Drain well and
leave to dry for a minute on the side
of the stove. Pass through a sieve or
Mouli, return the purée to the
saucepan and add:

2 oz. grated Parmesan
2 oz. flour
3 eggs
salt, pepper and nutmeg

Mix well and cool

Make into little rolls on a floured
board. Put them—a dozen at a time
into boiling salted water (do not boil
fiercely) for a few minutes until they
rise and are firm. Place on a dish in a
cool oven until they are all done, then
pour over melted butter and sprinkle
with grated Parmesan.

8

Patate all'Italiana

Wash and peel off a strip round eight
potatoes. Boil in salted water for
twenty minutes until cooked. Drain
them well and sieve them. Put them
back in the pan with

2 oz. butter
4 slices crustless bread
soaked in milk
½ cup milk
3 egg yolks
salt, pepper and nutmeg

Mix well together and add

3 beaten egg whites

Pile high in a baking dish, sprinkle
with melted butter and grated
Parmesan and bake until golden for
fifteen to twenty minutes.

9
Budino di patate con funghi

Boil eight potatoes, meanwhile, quarter and fry in butter add

1 lb. open mushrooms
salt and crushed peppercorns
2 tablespoons cream

Shake the pan and reserve until the potato purée is made

Drain and sieve the potatoes. Add

2 oz. butter
½ cup cream
3 egg yolks
salt and good pinch pepper

Butter a soufflé dish and put the purée in the bottom and sides leaving a well in the middle and some purée to put on top. Put the cooked mushrooms in the middle and seal with the rest of the purée. Cook for twenty minutes in the oven and turn out onto a dish (but leave in the dish if the potato has stuck to it).

Note. This potato purée can have a variety of fillings—leeks, spinach, small broad beans all mixed with a little cream.

10

Patate arrostite

Scrape three pounds of new equal-
sized round new potatoes

Heat   4 oz. butter
and   2 tablespoons olive oil
in a large deep frying-pan and
add   the potatoes, salt and pepper

Cover with a lid, place on a fairly
low fire and shake frequently. They
will take a good half hour and should
have a good brown crust.

11

Patate in stufato

Cut six large peeled potatoes into
approximately quarter-inch cubes.
Put them in a baking dish just
covered with milk. Sprinkle with
2 oz. butter, cover and bring to the
boil then put in a hot oven until
tender (still with the lid on).

I2

Patate Tartufate

Potatoes cooked with truffles and Parmesan

Slice four large potatoes fairly thin
and wash them in cold water. Lay
them in a buttered baking dish with
layers of potato, sliced Piedmontese
white truffles (if you can get them)
and grated Parmesan cheese. Finish
with grated Parmesan, sprinkle with
butter and lemon juice and moisten
with good chicken broth (about half
way up the baking dish). Bake in a
fairly hot oven until tender (about
forty minutes).

I3

Insalata di patate con vino e acciughe

Potato Salad with wine and anchovies

Mix six finely sliced cooked potatoes
with

**1 bunch spring onions,
chopped
1 glass red wine
salt and crushed pepper
1 cup olive oil
$\frac{1}{2}$ tablespoon wine vinegar
chopped chervil and parsley
twelve roughly chopped
anchovies**

Mix together and leave to marinate
before serving.

14

Insalata di patate   **Potato salad**

Slice six cooked potatoes. Slice 3
hard boiled eggs and mince 6 oz.
tunny fish. Place alternate layers of
potato, egg and minced tunny fish.
Pour over a *Vinaigrette* in which
there is chopped fresh fennel.

Pumpkin/*Zucca*

I

Zucche ripiene

Small pumpkins filled with tunny fish and spice, served with tomato sauce

Cut in half either three small American squashes (the size of your fist) or six large courgettes—about six inches long

Scoop out the insides with a dessertspoon, throwing away the seeds but preserving the pulp

Mix the pulp with

3 egg yolks
an 8-oz. tin of tunny fish with the oil
1 tablespoon grated Parmesan
pinch of allspice and pepper
small pinch salt

Fill the half pumpkin shells with the mixture. Sprinkle with more grated Parmesan and bake in a moderate oven with a lid

Serve with a tomato *coulis*, made simply by sweating

½ finely chopped onion in olive oil

When cooked, pour in add

1 tin Italian tomatoes
salt and pepper

Stew for twenty minutes and serve.

2
Zucche fritte

Strips of pumpkin or marrow fried in olive oil

Peel, halve and seed six courgettes (about six inches long) or one small pumpkin (smaller than a football). Cut the flesh into strips, the size of chips and leave them in a sieve sprinkled with salt for a couple of hours (to get rid of excess moisture)

Heat olive oil (or frying oil) in deep pan. Dip the strips in seasoned flour and fry until cooked and light brown

Drain well and serve at once, with a squeeze of lemon.

3
Zucche alla Fiorentina

Boil three small American squashes in salted water. When soft drain, cut in half and remove the seeds

In the middle put

**cream
a small knob of butter
salt, pepper and nutmeg
squeeze of lemon**

Bake in a hot oven for ten minutes

Sprinkle with chopped chives and serve.

Sorrel Purée/*Puré di acetosa*

The most practical way of using sorrel is to make it into a buttery purée which will keep in a glass jar in the refrigerator. This can then be used for a soup, a fish sauce, an omelette, mixed in with some young cooked peas, or with chopped cooked potatoes and cream.

Wash the sorrel carefully and put it into a pan with a little boiling water, season lightly and cover. Uncover and stir now and again until the sorrel is soft and a brownish colour (only three to four minutes). Drain and mix with melted butter. Keep in the refrigerator until needed.

Spinach/*Spinaci*

I
Spinaci al burro

Remove the stalks and wash two
pounds of spinach in a sink full of
cold water. Drain the spinach and
shred it.

In an earthenware pot put 2 oz.
butter and when this has melted add
the spinach, salt and pepper and a lid.
Stir constantly until the spinach is
cooked. If the spinach appears too wet
when almost cooked, remove the lid
and finish cooking until the juices
have evaporated.

2
Spinaci alla crema

Remove the stalks and wash two
pounds of spinach in a sink full of
cold water. Drain and chop it.

Melt 2 oz. butter in an earthenware
pot, and add the spinach, salt and
pepper. Cover with a lid removing
it to stir the spinach constantly. When
the spinach is cooked remove it
from the pan and let the juices
bubble.

Stir in 1 dessertspoon ($\frac{1}{2}$ oz.) flour and
$\frac{1}{4}$ pint cream, stir until it bubbles
and thickens, add the spinach and a
little grated nutmeg and 3 hard boiled
eggs roughly chopped. Reheat
thoroughly and serve.

3
Crocchette di spinaci

Remove the stalks and wash two
pounds of spinach in a sink full of
cold water. Drain well, chop and
put in an earthenware pot with salt
and pepper. Stir frequently and cover
with a lid. When cooked drain it and
press dry. Chop it again and replace
it in the earthenware pot with

4 oz. butter
a small bunch of marjoram,
chopped
1 teaspoon of sugar

and

a little grated zest of lemon

Mix well over the fire and put in

$\frac{1}{4}$ pint milk

When it boils add

2 beaten-up eggs

Remove from the fire and stir until
the egg thickens. Allow to cool. Then
roll into small sausages

Meanwhile make the batter:

Mix the oil and wine or water into

2 oz. flour
1 tablespoon olive oil
$\frac{1}{2}$ glass white wine (or
water)
salt

Roll the croquette in this batter
and deep fry

Serve with sections of lemon.

4

Ravioli alla Fiorentina

Remove the stalks and wash two pounds of spinach. Drain and cook in boiling salted water. When the water reboils, drain the spinach. Run cold water over it and press it very dry with the hands. Chop finely and put in a saucepan with

1 oz. flour
2 oz. butter
8 oz. fresh curd cheese (Ricotta)
3 egg yolks
salt, pepper and nutmeg
2 oz. grated Parmesan

Stir briskly for a minute or two and allow to cool. When cold roll into small pointed sausages (an inch long) flour them and lower them into boiling salted water. Simmer and as they rise remove them from the fire. Pour over melted butter, sprinkle with grated Parmesan and serve.

5

Spinaci in riccioli

Remove the stalks and wash one
pound of spinach, boil in salted
water for a few minutes, drain well.
Rub it through a sieve (alternatively
use frozen chopped spinach). Beat up
2 eggs with salt and pepper and mix
in the spinach

Pour a little olive oil into an
omelette- or pancake-pan, heat
thoroughly and pour in a little of
the mixture as for making a pancake,
i.e. as thin as possible. Turn it over,
take it out and repeat until all the
mixture is used, stacking the pancakes
on top of one another

Shred the pancakes into fingers and
pour a purée of tomatoes (simply
tomatoes and seasoning sweated in
oil with a lid on and then passed
through a sieve) over them and
sprinkle with Parmesan. Brown in a
hot oven

Good with smoked sausages or the
pancakes shredded into consommé.

6

Sformato di spinaci

Spinach soufflé

Wash, cook and sieve	2 lb. spinach
heat in a saucepan	1½ oz. butter
add and cook	1½ oz. flour
add and bring to the boil	¼ pint thin cream
season with	salt, pepper and nutmeg
mix in without boiling	2 egg yolks
when cool, whisk and fold in	3 egg whites

Half fill individual soufflé dishes.
Sprinkle well with Parmesan and bake
in a moderate to hot oven for ten to
fifteen minutes depending on the size
of the dish.

Serve, needless to say, at once.

Note. If this is cooked for a party,
prepare the soufflé base ahead with
all but the egg whites in it. The base
should be warm but not hot or cold.
Whip and fold in the egg whites so
that the soufflé will be cooked when
you wish to eat.

7

Sformato di spinaci con funghi

Either make a purée of spinach (as in
spinace in Riccioli) or heat two half-
pound packets of frozen spinach purée
in

2 oz. butter

Cook until fairly dry. Add the
juice of

$\frac{1}{2}$ **a lemon**

Leave to cool. Beat up
with

3 egg yolks
one whole egg

Butter a mould—preferably a ring
mould but if not, a soufflé dish. Add
the spinach to the egg and the
mixture to the mould. Cook *au bain
marie* for an hour in a moderate oven
and when set, turn out and pour
mushrooms fried with a little garlic
and finished with tomatoes and
seasoning into the middle.

Tomato/*Pomodori*

I
Conserva di pomodori   **Tomato conserve**

Wash as many ripe or nearly ripe
(not over ripe) tomatoes as you wish.
Put them in a deep saucepan, sprinkle
with salt and pepper and sugar, put
on a lid and cook slowly, stirring
from time to time until the tomatoes
are a pulp

Pass the pulp through a Mouli or
sieve and preserve in jars or keep it
in a refrigerator with olive oil on top
or, in these days of large deep freezes,
pour the cold purée into polythene
bags and freeze until needed

This purée is a basic ingredient to
much of Italian cooking. It is used in
soups, risottos, sauces and many meat
dishes.

2

Pomodori alla griglia alla senape

Grilled tomatoes with a mustard dressing

Halve six large ripe tomatoes without skinning them and put them to grill cut side up with salt, pepper and a brushing of olive oil

While they are grilling baste with a dressing of

1 tablespoon olive oil
juice of ½ a lemon
small teaspoon sugar
small teaspoon French mustard
little salt and pepper

Place the tomatoes in a hot dish with the dressing. Sprinkle with parsley.

3

Pomodori al forno

Cut six large ripe tomatoes in half without skinning them. Scoop out some of the pips and centre with a teaspoon. Prepare a stuffing with sweated in

six sliced mushrooms
1 tablespoon olive oil
chopped small clove of garlic
pinch of chopped parsley
pinch of chopped chives

Fill the tomatoes with the stuffing and sprinkle with Parmesan

Bake for ten to fifteen minutes.

4
Pomodori alla panna

Scald and peel twelve small ripe
tomatoes

Heat in an earthenware pan	**1 tablespoon olive oil**
sweat without colour	**1 chopped onion**
add	**1 tablespoon chopped fresh**
	marjoram
	½ oz. flour
Cook for a minute and add	**salt and pepper**
	¼ pint thin cream

Bring the cream to the boil, shaking
the pan occasionally. Add the
tomatoes and cook on top or
in the very hot oven for five minutes
or until the tomatoes are cooked.
Serve sprinkled with chopped
parsley.

5

Pomodori con uova

Take six large tomatoes, cut off the
top and keep it aside to make a lid.
Scoop out the middle carefully and
break an egg into each tomato.
Season with salt and pepper and a
little chopped tarragon, add a nut of
butter and replace the tomato lid.
Place the tomatoes on a well buttered
dish and season them lightly. Bake in
a very hot oven until the eggs are set
(10–12 minutes)

The tomatoes can be served on a
round base of buttered toast covered
with a slice of ham

Other tomato stuffings:

**1) left over risotto
2) chopped anchovies, olives
garlic and breadcrumbs
3) chopped mushrooms and
shrimps
4) flaked cooked smoked
haddock—serve with garlic
mayonnaise**

6

Gelatina di pomodori   Tomato jelly

Heat one pint of tomato preserve

Add

**1 tablespoon finely chopped
chives
juice of a lemon to taste
pinch of cayenne**

Pour over

**one $\frac{1}{2}$ oz. packet of dissolved
gelatine**

and pour into a ring mould

Turn out when set and fill the centre
with fresh prawns mixed with a little
mayonnaise.

7

Insalata di pomodori   **Tomato salads**

a) Slice six tomatoes (peeled first or not, according to your wish) and dress with

**1 tablespoon tarragon
vinegar
2 tablespoons good olive oil
sprinkling of sugar and salt
chopped chives**

b) Scald and peel six tomatoes. Halve them and scoop out the seeds (keep them for a soup or stew). Fill the tomatoes with chopped hard boiled egg mixed with mayonnaise and chopped tarragon.

c) Slice the tomatoes. Chop some celery very finely and sprinkle over them. Pour over some *Vinaigrette* dressing.

d) Slice the tomatoes and make a lattice work over them with thin strips of anchovy. Roughly chop some stoned black olives and sprinkle over. Pour over a little *Vinaigrette* dressing to which has been added a little crushed garlic.

e) Choose large tomatoes, peel them (if preferred) and slice them lengthways. Alternate the slices of tomatoes with slices of peeled Italian peach, overlapping well. Season with salt and pepper, sprinkle lemon juice over and a little walnut oil.

Mixed Vegetables and Salads

I

Sformato di verdura

Flan of vegetables
baked vegetable cake

Use a total of	3 lb. mixed vegetables
of which there should be	1 lb. potatoes
Prepare them and cut them up fairly small. Put them in a saucepan with	2 oz. melted butter 1 cup water salt and pepper 1 bunch sweet herbs
Cover with a lid and stew gently until cooked. Then add	1 cup cream
Stir and leave to cool	
Mix in	4 yolks of eggs 4 oz. grated cheese
and fold in	4 beaten egg whites

Put the mixture in a buttered mould,
well lined with breadcrumbs,
cover with more breadcrumbs and a
buttered paper and bake in a
moderate oven for forty minutes.

2

Verdure miste brasate

Mixed braised vegetables (a winter dish)

Prepare the following vegetables, cutting the carrots, turnips and leeks into three-inch strips

$\frac{1}{4}$ lb. small onions
$\frac{1}{2}$ lb. carrots
$\frac{1}{4}$ lb. turnips
$\frac{1}{2}$ lb. leeks
$\frac{1}{2}$ lb. celery
1 medium cabbage

Arrange the onions, carrots, turnips and leeks in a large shallow oven dish. Almost
add

cover with stock
salt and pepper
pinch of mixed herbs

Braise in a moderate oven for half an hour.

Meanwhile, blanch the cabbage for five minutes in boiling salted water. Drain and cut into six pieces, each with a little stalk; arrange the cabbage with the other vegetables. Cook for a further twenty minutes.

Sprinkle with plenty of parsley. Take care that the vegetables are not over-cooked for the flavour will lose freshness and become 'gassy'.

3

Cappon magro

A mixture of spring
vegetables, piled up into
a pyramid.
Serve with a plain roast

This mixture can vary a good deal
but this list will indicate some of the
range of choice. Use at least six of
them:

small new potatoes
small onions
baby carrots
small french beans
courgettes
bulb fennel
small sliced artichokes
broad beans
asparagus
baby cauliflower
small peas
tomatoes

The only rule to follow is that the
root vegetables should be cooked
separately, starting with cold water.
The others in boiling water.

The vegetables, when cooked and
drained are mixed together and
tossed in melted butter and more salt
and pepper.

4
Fritto misto   **Mixed fried vegetables**

Traditionally, this is a dish of fried vegetables with fried calves brains and chicken rissoles. The following recipe, however, omits the meat.

Prepare the following vegetables:

Pare, cut into slices and keep in cold water	**6 young artichokes**
Top and tail and cut into long ¼ in. strips	**4 small courgettes**
Quarter and take out the seeds of	**3 red peppers**
Blanch, for five minutes and separate into flowers	**1 small cauliflower**
Finally fill, with the following stuffing	**twelve courgettes flowers**
Clean, cook and squeeze dry mix in	**1 lb. spinach** **3 demi-sel cheeses** **1 egg** **salt, pepper and nutmeg**

Fry all these vegetables, in stages, in deep fat, first dipping them in the following batter:

Put in a bowl and make a well with	**4 oz. flour** **salt and pepper**
In the well, put	**2 egg yolks** **3 tablespoons olive oil**
Start mixing in the flour and gradually add until it is smooth and like thick cream	**½ pint water**
Finally, add	**2 beaten egg whites**

Mixed Salads/*Insalate miste*

I
alla Cardinale

Wash a lettuce and a bunch of watercress	
Cut into strips	**3 small beetroot**
Quarter	**3 hard boiled eggs**
Wash	**twelve radishes**
Slice	**½ cucumber**
Arrange them all on a shallow dish and serve with a creamy mayonnaise:	
Put, in a bowl	**2 egg yolks**
Very gradually add and	**¼ pint olive oil** **1 dessertspoon white wine vinegar**
Add and	**salt and pepper** **2 tablespoons cream**

2

all' Italiana

Cook	1 lb. new potatoes in their skins
and	½ lb. baby carrots

Peel the potatoes. When cold, cut the potatoes and carrots into slices.

Then cut into 2 in. lengths, then in half and then shred very finely	2 washed leeks

Mix the vegetables together with the following Sauce Lombarda:

In a bowl, put very gradually add	2 egg yolks ¼ pint olive oil salt and pepper 1 dessertspoon lemon juice 1 dessertspoon tomato purée 1 dessertspoon chopped fresh herbs

3

alla Macedone

Mix together	½ lb. cooked french beans ½ lb. cooked young peas ¼ lb. soaked and cooked haricot beans

Dress with the following *Vinaigrette*—the olive oil should be the finest:	2 tablespoons wine vinegar salt and pepper 1 tablespoon chopped chives 4 tablespoons olive oil

4
alla pollastra

Arrange on a dish the following:

2 sliced peppers
6 tomatoes quartered
the remains of a cold
chicken
1 small Cos lettuce shredded
24 stoned olives

Make a *Vinaigrette* sauce with salt,
pepper, sugar, vinegar and olive oil
and add a little cream. Pour over the
salad.

5
alla Russa

**Mixed salad with prawns,
capers, anchovies and
mock caviare dressing**

Cut up and mix together cooked

**asparagus
french beans
peas
young carrots**

add

**some capers
anchovies
prawns**

Pour over a sauce made with

**salt and cayenne pepper
1 teaspoon mustard
½ grated onion
small jar Danish 'caviare'
3 tablespoons vinegar
6 tablespoons olive oil**

Rice/*Riso*

Cooking Rice

Wash the rice and pour it into plenty of boiling salted water. Stir the rice until the water reboils, and continue boiling for about a quarter of an hour until the rice is just soft between the teeth. Drain it in a colander and rinse briefly under hot water, serve or put in a buttered casserole, cover with a lid and keep hot—but not too hot.

Pilafs and Risottos

The basic difference between a pilaf and a risotto is firstly the amount of liquid in which the fried rice is cooked. Pilaf should be dry and have the same quantity of liquid as of rice, a risotto should be moist and needs half as much liquid again as a pilaf. Secondly, whereas a pilaf is a plain, flavoured rice dish (say with saffron or herbs) usually served as an accompaniment; a risotto has a high proportion of additional ingredients, making it a dish in itself. The commonest mistake with a risotto is to have too high a proportion of rice.

The rice in pilafs and risottos should be fried first in the best olive oil obtainable. Pilafs and risottos should 'repose' for a few minutes once they are cooked. The rice, during this time absorbs more moisture.

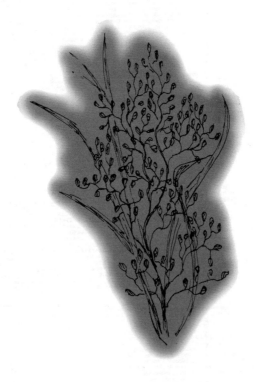

I
Pilaf

Fry, in an earthenware pot	½ finely chopped onion
in	2 tablespoons good olive oil
add and fry	8 oz. rice
add	1¼ pint stock or water and bouillon cube
	1 bay leaf
	salt and pepper if necessary

Bring to the boil, cover and simmer gently on top of the stove or in a moderate oven for nearly half an hour until the rice is cooked. Remove this from the stove and leave without a lid in a warm place or oven for a few minutes and serve.

2
Riso alla Ristori

In an earthenware casserole put	4 oz. green bacon, chopped
	1 chopped onion
	¼ to ½ shredded white cabbage
	a little salt, pepper and sugar
	6 slices garlic sausage, quartered
Cover with a lid and stew for half an hour, add	4 oz. Italian or Patna rice
	¾ pint stock
	1 tablespoon chopped parsley

Simmer gently for a further twenty minutes and serve with grated Parmesan.

3
Riso al pomodoro

In an earthenware casserole put add	2 tablespoons olive oil 1 finely chopped onion 1 chopped clove garlic
and stew without colouring	
Add and fry add	8 oz. Italian rice 1 tablespoon chopped marjoram 1 pint tomato pulp (see p. 120) salt and pepper

Bring to the boil, simmer for about twenty minutes until the rice is almost cooked, remove from the fire and leave to rest for five minutes before serving with grated Parmesan.

4
Risotto ai funghi secchi — Rice with dried cèpes

In a small bowl soak in warm water	2 oz. dried cèpes
In an earthenware casserole heat	2 tablespoons olive oil
Add and fry without colouring and	1 finely chopped onion 1 good clove of garlic chopped
Add and fry	6 oz. Avorio rice
Add the soaked and chopped	cèpes pinch of thyme 1 pint stock or water and chicken bouillon cube mill ground pepper

Bring to the boil, simmer gently for twenty to twenty-five minutes. Leave to rest for five minutes and sprinkle with parsley and cheese.

5

Risotto ai gamberi	**Risotto with prawns**
In an earthenware casserole put	2 tablespoons olive oil
Add and fry without colouring and	1 finely chopped onion 1 chopped clove garlic
Then add and fry and	6 oz. Italian rice twelve good-sized Mediterranean prawns in their shells
Add	1 level dessertspoon of tomato purée juice of a lemon pinch of mixed herbs pinch of cayenne 1 pint water with chicken bouillon cube

Bring to the boil, simmer in a moderate oven with a lid for nearly twenty minutes until the rice is just soft to the bite. Put the risotto to one side to 'repose', correct the seasoning and serve.

6

Riso pilaf allo zafferano	Saffron Pilaf
In an earthenware casserole put	2 tablespoons olive oil
Add and fry without colour add and	1 finely chopped onion 8 oz. Italian or Patna rice ½ coffee-spoon crushed saffron
Fry the rice and add and the	1 pint stock juice of one lemon
Bring to the boil, cover with a lid and simmer in the oven or on top for about twenty minutes until the rice is really cooked. Take off the heat and leave it to stand for five minutes.	

7

Risotto alla Poggio Gherardo	Risotto with marsala and chicken livers
In an earthenware casserole heat	2 tablespoons olive oil
Add and fry	1 chopped onion 6 oz. rice
Then add	1 port glass marsala
Let it bubble almost dry and add and	1 pint chicken stock small pinch of mixed herbs good pinch crushed pepper
Then add	4 chopped chicken livers (roughly 4 oz.)
Simmer for twenty minutes. Let the rice rest for five minutes and serve with grated Parmesan.	

8

Risotto alla Milanese

In an earthenware casserole heat and	2 tablespoons olive oil 1 oz. butter
In this fry golden	1 chopped onion
Add	6 oz. sliced mushrooms a large pinch crushed saffron (1 chopped truffle)
Stir in and fry	6 oz. Avorio rice
Add and	1 pint chicken stock 1½ oz. grated Parmesan

Simmer for eighteen minutes. Let it rest and serve with grated Parmesan.

9

Crocchette di riso e spinaci   For using cooked rice

Mix together	8 tablespoons cooked rice 1 lb. cooked spinach squeezed dry and chopped 2 eggs ground nutmeg salt and pepper 1 oz. grated Parmesan grated rind of one lemon

Bind, if too soft, with a little flour. Then with floured hands roll into sausages on a floured board and dip in beaten egg and breadcrumbs and fry golden.

Macaroni/*Pasta Asciutta*

Making *pasta* is not difficult nor does it take too long but space in the form of a good-sized kitchen table is essential for rolling out the paste as thin as paper. In Italy there always seem to be a few black clad grand-mothers and aunts who have the build for kneading and the time to spare.

The commercial pasta, however, is fairly good—except for perhaps with *lasagne* and *ravioli* where the fresh pasta is noticeably better. Some fifty varieties are presented in the catalogues of pasta manufacturers; tubes, shells, rods, nuts and bolts, the whole display having the appearance of an ironmonger's advertisement.

The commercial *lasagne* needs blanching for ten to fifteen minutes, unlike the home-made which only needs five minutes in boiling salted water. The *fettucini* and macaroni to be served simply with butter and cheese or with a sauce will need a little more than fifteen minutes depend-ing on its shape and size. When cooked, it should be *al dente*—with a slight bite to it. Someone I know, hurls a strand of spaghetti at the wall and if it sticks, it is cooked.

To make Pasta

In a basin put	**1 lb. plain flour**
Make a well and break in	**3 eggs**
Add	**1 scant teaspoon salt**
Break up the eggs with a wooden spoon and gradually incorporate the flour gradually adding about	**4 fluid oz. water**

Then knead until elastic (about five minutes). Divide the paste and roll out paper thin until just about transparent, dusting lightly and frequently with flour. Leave to rest for half an hour and then cut as required into oblongs for *lasagne* and *cannelloni*; small squares for ravioli or rolled and shredded for *tagliatelle*.

I

Fettucine alla crema

'Ribbons' served with cheese and cream

Stick an onion with a clove and cook it with one pound of *fettucini* or *tagliatelle* in boiling salted water for nearly twenty minutes. When just cooked, drain well and remove the onion

Return to the saucepan with

2 oz. butter
4 oz. grated Emmenthal
2 oz. grated Parmesan
pinch of nutmeg
a little grated nutmeg
6 fluid oz. cream

Cook for a few minutes over a low flame until the cheese melts and becomes elastic. Serve very hot.

2

Maccheroni al forno

Lasagne baked with mozzarella cheese

Blanch one pound of *lasagne* in boiling salted water or stock for fifteen minutes until just soft. Meanwhile, slice two *mozzarella* cheeses thinly (these can be bought in Soho). Drain the pasta when cooked and refresh under running hot water. In a thick baking dish alternate the pasta with layers of cheese, seasoned with ground pepper, nutmeg and grated Parmesan. Finish with pasta, sprinkle with grated Parmesan, breadcrumbs and a few small nuts of butter, bake in a hot oven until brown and sizzling. (Beware, the *mozzarella* will be extremely elastic.)

3

Spaghetti alla Napoletana

A sauce of mushrooms (white truffles) tongue and tomatoes

Cook one pound of spaghetti for nearly twenty minutes until just soft. Drain it well and return it to the saucepan and pour over the following sauce:

In a small saucepan heat	1 tablespoon olive oil
Add and fry, without colour	1 small chopped onion
Add and cook	¼ lb. chopped mushrooms
Then add	1 small tin of tomatoes, crushed salt and pepper a little chopped white truffle 2 oz. chopped tongue

Simmer gently for five minutes, serve very hot and also with grated Parmesan.

4

Spaghetti alla Quaresima   **Spaghetti with parsley,
anchovies and white wine**

Boil one pound of spaghetti in
salted water for about twenty minutes
until just soft. Drain well and serve
with the following sauce:

Heat, in a small saucepan	**1 tablespoon olive oil**
In it, fry golden,	**1 large chopped onion** **1 clove chopped garlic** **8 chopped anchovies** **1 glass white wine**
Reduce the wine and add	**8 fluid oz. fish stock (from** **a turbot or cod's head) or** **water**
Season with	**a pinch of white pepper** **2 tablespoons chopped** **parsley**

Serve this sauce with the spaghetti
and a bowl of grated Parmesan.
Flaked fish, prawns, mussels or squid
can be added to the sauce.

5

Maccheroni alla Siciliana

Lasagne cooked with chopped cooked veal, ham, eggs and herbs

Blanch three-quarters of a pound of *lasagne* for fifteen minutes until nearly soft, drain and refresh under hot running water

Meanwhile chop

and

1 lb. cooked veal (beef or lamb will do)
4 oz. ham

Slice
and chop

4 hard-boiled eggs
2 tablespoons marjoram, chives, little basil and chervil

Butter a baking dish (a fairly shallow casserole). Lay pieces of *pasta* on the bottom, then meat, eggs, herbs and seasoning, more *pasta*, another layer of meat etc, and finally a layer of *pasta*

Pour in enough

stock or water with chicken bouillon

nearly to cover.

Sprinkle with grated Parmesan and a few small nuts of butter and bake in a hot oven for twenty minutes until browned.

6

Timballo ai funghi

Cooked *fettucini* coiled inside a mould filled with *fettucini* and mushroom sauce; then baked

---

Cook one pound of *fettucini* in boiling salted water until nearly soft. Drain and allow to cool. Butter a timbale mould or pudding basin (about seven inches in diameter)

Meanwhile prepare the following sauce:

Melt in a frying pan	2 oz. butter
add	1 chopped clove garlic
and	8 oz. sliced button mushrooms

Cook until the moisture of the mushrooms has evaporated and add	1 oz. flour
Mix in and add	½ pint good stock 1 tablespoon chopped marjoram salt and pepper

Simmer for ten minutes

Coil some of the cool *fettucini* round the inside of the timbale well packed and slightly overlapping until the sides and base are covered. Mix the sauce with the remainder of the *fettucini* and pour into the middle of the mould. Put the mould in a baking dish of water, cover the mould with a saucer and place in a moderate oven for forty minutes

Turn out carefully on to a hot dish and serve with grated Parmesan and a fresh purée of tomatoes (twelve tomatoes squashed into a saucepan, seasoned, covered and stewed for ten minutes and then passed through the Mouli).

7

Pappardelle con lepre	Wide noodles with hare sauce

Cook some wide strip noodles (wider than *fettucini*) in boiling salted water until nearly soft (about twenty minutes), drain and mix with the following sauce made from legs and shoulder of hare. (Use the saddle of hare for roasting.)

In a thick frying pan heat	1 tablespoon olive oil
Add	4 oz. streaky bacon chopped ½ chopped onion 1 clove garlic chopped 1 chopped piece of celery
When brown add the small pieces of	chopped hare
Rolled in	seasoned flour
Brown the hare and add and	1 glass red wine 1 glass stock
Season with	thyme salt and pepper

Cover the pan and cook slowly for an hour

Shake the sauce and pour into a bowl and serve with the noodles.

8

Agnolotti alla Poggio Gherardo   Home-made Ravioli with minced chicken (truffle), butter and cream

Mince finely, twice sweat in	1½ lb. cooked chicken ½ chopped onion 4 oz. butter
Stir butter and onion into the chicken and add	salt and pepper pinch of tarragon (1 chopped white truffle optional) 1 sherry glass of dry white vermouth 4 fluid oz. cream (single)

Work the mixture to a paste

Make a pound of pasta (see p. 138) divide it and roll it paper thin. Leave it to rest for half an hour and then put teaspoonfuls of the chicken mixture on one piece of pasta at about two-inch distances, brush very lightly in between with egg-wash and lay the second sheet of pasta lightly on top. Press down round the little heaps and then cut out with a knife or one of those small scooped wheels.

Have ready a large saucepan of boiling salted water and put in it the ravioli. Boil slowly for about eight minutes, take them out with a strainer, season with melted butter and Parmesan cheese. Serve very hot.

9

Crescioni

Little pasta turnovers filled with spinach, herbs and cream and deep fried

Wash and boil | 1½ lb. spinach

Drain well, pressing the spinach dry with the back of a wooden spoon. Roughly chop the spinach and put it in a frying-pan with

3 tablespoons very good olive oil
2 small cloves garlic, chopped
grated nutmeg
salt and pepper
1 tablespoon fresh chopped herbs such as marjoram, chervil and chives
2 tablespoons grated Parmesan

Mix the spinach and the ingredients, simmer for five minutes, remove from the stove and leave to cool

Meanwhile make pasta as described on p. 138 and roll it out thin as paper, leave it to rest for half an hour and cut into three-inch squares. (Thinly rolled puff pastry will also do quite well.) Put a little heap of spinach on one square at a time and fold over like a turnover, brushing the edges with egg-wash. Seal the edges firmly and, when they are all prepared, deep fry them for three minutes on each side in not too hot oil until lightly coloured. Dust with grated Parmesan and serve on a napkin with a fresh purée of tomatoes (twelve ripe tomatoes squashed into a saucepan, seasoned, covered and stewed for ten minutes, pass through the Mouli).

10

Tagliatelle alla Romagnola

Thin strip noodles
fettucini, **with garlic,
tomatoes and small garlic
sausages**

Cook a pound of *fettucini* or home-
made pasta, cut into strips, in boiling
salted water until just soft (fifteen to
twenty minutes). Meanwhile make
the following sauce with sausages

In a thick frying-pan heat

3 tablespoons olive oil

In it fry gently

**3 cloves garlic, chopped
parsley
twelve small fresh garlic
sausages or good butcher's
sausages**

When the sausages are nearly cooked
add

**1 tin tomatoes (14–16 oz.)
salt and pepper to taste**

Let the sauce and sausages stew for
ten minutes

Drain the *fettucini* and lay in a dish
making a well in the middle. Arrange
the sausages and sauce in the middle
and sprinkle with grated Parmesan.
Serve very hot.

Soups/Zuppe

Almost all the soups in this book have a basic form of onion and potato, a further vegetable and stock added later. Potato, I find, is a better thickening for soup than flour partly because it is a vegetable itself and not a cereal and also because the consistency is fresher and more palatable. Today the use of electric blenders, which save much time and labour, has revived the serving of delicious home-made soups.

I

Minestra di asparagi	Asparagus Soup

It would be extravagant to use
bunches of asparagus just for soup
unless you have a garden with weak
shoots that are too thin to eat as a
vegetable or can buy the sprue
asparagus from the shops. Ideal,
however, is to use the trimmings
from asparagus when they are to be
prepared as a vegetable, those white
stalky ends

Cut off, then, the thick white stalks
of the asparagus (about one third of
the length) and wash them. (Boil the
green parts as recommended in the
asparagus section but reserve a few
tips for garnishing the soup.)
Alternatively use two pounds of
sprue, reserve and boil the very tips
and use the rest for the soup

In a thick-based saucepan
melt   **2 oz. butter**
add   **1 small onion, chopped**
and   **3 medium potatoes, peeled and sliced**

and the   **asparagus trimmings or sprue**

Season lightly with   **salt and pepper**
and cover with a lid

Sweat for fifteen minutes, remove
the lid and add   **2 pints milk**

Stir and add a small bunch of   **parsley**

Bring to the boil and simmer for
fifteen minutes. Pass through a fine
Mouli or seive. Return to a saucepan,
bring to the boil, correct the
seasoning and the consistency with a
little cream and garnish with tops of
asparagus. Serve with fried crôutons.

2

Minestra di cavolo e maiale   Cabbage and pork Soup

This, as with many soups is open to
different combinations but be careful
with this soup (as, indeed, with any
other vegetable soup) that it is not
over-cooked for the flavour becomes
stale.

Remove the stalk from   ½ small white cabbage or
                                      ¼ large one

Cut the cabbage in two or three
slices and shred it finely

Finely chop   ½ lb. piece salt streaky or
                                      mild, streaky bacon

Put it in a saucepan with   1 tablespoon dripping or
                                      butter

Lightly fry the bacon with   1 shredded onion
add the   shredded cabbage
and   freshly milled pepper

Stir the cabbage over the fire for a
few minutes and then add   2 pints stock or water

Bring to the boil and simmer for   twenty minutes

Skim from time to time. A few
minutes before serving correct the
seasoning and add   1 finely sliced cooking apple
and/or a few   crushed chestnuts

3

Minestra di carote	Carrot Soup

In a thick pan (with a lid) melt add	2 oz. butter 1 roughly chopped onion 4 large peeled and chopped carrots 1 small peeled and chopped turnip twelve crushed coriander seeds
Season lightly with	salt and pepper
Cover with a lid and heat gently for twenty minutes, then add	2 pints stock or water and chicken bouillon
Bring to the boil and simmer for twelve minutes. Pass the soup through a medium mesh Mouli or strainer, return to the saucepan and reboil. Correct the seasoning and consistency with a little more stock and finish with	½ cup chopped herbs (a combination of chives, parsley, chervil, marjoram, thyme or rosemary)

Serve with fried crôutons.

4

Minestra di cetriolo alla crema	Cucumber and cream Soup

| Peel strips of skin from and liquidise with

and | 1 cucumber
1 large or 2 small dill pickled cucumbers
juice of a lemon
½ onion grated |
| After liquidising stir in | 6 fluid oz. cream
salt and pepper
1 tablespoon chopped dill |

If necessary add a squeeze of lemon juice. Keep chilled and serve with a little diced cucumber in the soup.

5

Minestra di lenti

Lentil Soup
(It is important to have a
good chicken or meat
stock for this soup)

Soak half a pound of lentils for a few
hours in warm water

Into a saucepan, put

1 onion roughly chopped
1 chopped stick of celery
1 carrot finely chopped
½ lb. brown lentils (soaked)
4 pints good stock

Bring to the boil and simmer for an
hour to an hour and a half, until the
lentils are soft. The stock will have
reduced by about a pint. Skim, and
season with the following mixture:

In a bowl mix

6 finely chopped anchovies
1 chopped clove of garlic
2 tablespoons chopped
parsley
6 leaves sage, chopped
4 fluid oz. good olive oil
twelve roughly crushed
peppercorns

Stir this mixture well into the soup;
remove from the fire and allow to
rest (the lentils will absorb some of
the oil). Reheat before serving and mix
well.

6

Minestra di lattuga

Lettuce Soup
**(A good summer soup hot
or cold, but if served cold
reduce the amount of
potato. Use lettuces that
remain underdeveloped in
the garden, the leaves of
ones that have just bolted
or the outside leaves of
about three lettuces)**

In a saucepan melt
add

and

2 oz. butter
**1 medium sized onion,
chopped**
**3 medium peeled and diced
potatoes**

Cover with a lid and stew gently for
twenty minutes

Remove the lid and add

**2 pints chicken stock or
water and chicken bouillon**

Bring to the boil and add the

**roughly chopped lettuce
leaves**
a small bunch of chervil
pepper and salt (if necessary)

Boil for ten minutes and then pass
through the fine Mouli. Return to
the saucepan and before serving add

6 oz. cream (thin)
chopped chives and chervil

7

Minestra di piselli	**Pea Soup** **(An easy soup to make** **using the pods and the** **peas but a good Mouli is** **essential)**

In a saucepan put

3 lb. peas in their pods
roughly crushed
1 grated onion
small bunch sweet herbs

Add

3 pints boiling water
salt and pepper

Bring to the boil and boil uncovered
for half an hour. Boil fiercely to keep
the colour of the peas. Pass the soup
through a coarse Mouli and then
through the fine. Return to the
saucepan and reboil for five minutes

Correct the seasoning, add
and serve with fried bread crôutons.

3 tablespoons thick cream

8

Minestra di zucca	**Pumpkin Soup** **(A spiced soup)**
Peel and roughly dice a	**2 lb. slice of yellow** **pumpkin**
Put it in a saucepan with and	**2 oz. butter** **1 chopped onion** **twelve coriander seeds** **large pinch cumin** **salt and ground pepper** **1 medium potato peeled and** **chopped**
Cover with a lid and simmer for twenty minutes. Remove the lid, add	**3 pints stock or water and** **chicken bouillon**
Bring to the boil and simmer for thirty minutes, uncovered. Pass the soup through the coarse disc of the Mouli, return to the pan and reboil. Check the seasoning and add fresh milled pepper a small spoonful of cream for each bowl and chopped parsley.	

9

Cream of Onion soup

Melt, in a saucepan	**2 oz. butter**
Peel and chop	**5 medium-sized onions**
Put the onions in the saucepan with	**3 peeled and diced potatoes (medium sized)** **salt, pepper and nutmeg**
Cover with a lid and stew gently for add and bring to the boil	**twenty minutes** **2 pints chicken stock**
Boil for ten minutes and pass through a fine Mouli. Return to the saucepan and add	**½ pint single cream**

Correct the seasoning and garnish
with chopped parsley and fried bread
croûtons.

IO

Minestra di carciofi di Giudea   Jerusalem Artichoke Soup

Peel and slice into a bowl of cold water (with a piece of lemon)	**6 good-sized Jerusalem artichokes**
Peel and chop	**1 onion**
Melt, in a saucepan	**2 oz. butter**
Add the onion and Jerusalem artichoke and season lightly with	**salt and pepper**
Cover with a lid and simmer gently for ten minutes	
Remove the lid and add	**2 pints of milk**
Bring to the boil. Simmer gently for a further ten minutes and pass the soup through the fine Mouli. Return the soup to the saucepan. Reboil and correct the seasoning, add a little	**single cream chopped chervil**
and fried bread croûtons, before serving.	

II

Polentina alla Veneziana   Maize-flour Soup

Bring to the boil and skim	**3 pints good chicken broth**
Mix into a little of the stock	**3 tablespoons polenta (fine maize flour)**
Stir to a paste	
Stir the paste carefully into the stock then gradually add	**3 oz. butter**
Serve with fried bread croûtons.	

12

Minestra di acetosa	Sorrel Soup

In a saucepan melt	2 oz. butter
add	2 peeled and chopped onions
and	3 peeled and chopped potatoes
Season with	salt and pepper
Cover with a lid, simmer gently for twenty minutes. Remove the lid and add	3 pints chicken stock $\frac{1}{2}$ lb. washed sorrel

Bring to the boil and simmer for five minutes. Pass through a coarse Mouli and serve with croûtons and a little cream added to each bowl of soup.

13

Minestra di crescione	Watercress Soup

In a saucepan melt	2 oz. butter
add	1 onion peeled and chopped
	3 medium sized potatoes
and the stalks of	3 bunches watercress
Cover with a lid and season with and stew gently for twenty minutes. Remove the lid and add and the remainder of the watercress. Bring to the boil and cook for ten minutes, pass through the medium Mouli and return to the saucepan and add	salt and pepper

2 pints chicken stock

$\frac{1}{2}$ pint single cream |

Correct the seasoning and consistency. Garnish with chopped parsley.

14

Minestra di spinaci	Spinach Soup

Into put and	3 pints chicken stock 2 medium sized potatoes (peeled and sliced) 1 bunch chopped spring onions
Bring to the boil and cook for twenty minutes and add	1 lb. spinach, washed and roughly chopped

and a little grated nutmeg. Cook for
a further ten minutes. Pass through a
coarse Mouli and season. Finish with
a little cream cheese softened with
cream.

15

Minestra di pomodori	Tomato Soup

In a saucepan melt add and	2 oz. butter 1 onion peeled and chopped 1 medium-sized potato, peeled and chopped
Cover with a lid and simmer gently for twenty minutes	
Remove the lid and add and	3 lb. ripe tomatoes 1 pint chicken stock (or to make a quick soup— 1 large tin Italian peeled tomatoes)

Bring to the boil and simmer for ten
minutes, pass through a medium
mouli and return to the saucepan.
Re-season adding a pinch of sugar
and garnish with a little chopped
basil, marjoram or parsley.

16

Minestra di verdura, erbe e crema	Vegetable, herb and cream Soup

Into a saucepan melt	2 oz. butter
add	2 chopped sticks celery
	1 chopped leek
	1 chopped carrot
Season with salt and pepper, cover with a lid and stew gently for twenty minutes. Add	3 pints chicken stock
	1 roughly chopped lettuce
	¼ lb. sorrel or spinach, washed and chopped
Bring to the boil and simmer for ten minutes. Pass through the medium Mouli and return to the saucepan. Reboil, correct the seasoning and add	3 tablespoons chopped herbs (which might include, chervil, chives, marjoram and a little thyme or tarragon)
Add a little cream before serving.	

Index

Mushroom (s) *(continued)*
  rolls stuffed with, 90
  salad, 90
  and tarragon cream, 88
  with tomatoes and garlic, 89

Noodles, 138–147 *(see also* Ribbon noodles)
  how to make, 138
  kinds of, 138

Onions, 91–92
  baked herbed, 91
  baked stuffed, 91
  cream of onion soup, 156
  fried, 92
  glazed, 92

Pappardelle con lepre, 144
Parmesan sauce, 13
Parsnips, 93–94
  cooked with butter, 93
  deep-fried, 94
  Parmesan, au gratin, 94
Pasta, 138–147 *(see also* Fettucini; Lasagne; Ravioli; Ribbon noodles; Spaghetti; Tagliatelle)
  how to make, 138
  kinds of, 138
Pasta turnovers, spinach-filled, 146
Pastinace, 93–94
  al burro, 93

Pastinace *(continued)*
  al forno, 94
  fritte, 94
Patate, 100–110
  arrostite, 108
  alla Borghese, 100
  budino di, con funghi, 107·
  alla campagnuola, 100
  in casseruola, 101
  alla crema, 102
  crocchette di, 103
  al forno, 104
  gnocchi di, 105
  insalata di, 110
    con vino e acciughe, 109
  all'Italiana, 106
  in stufato, 108
  Tartufate, 108
Peas, 20, 95–97
  choice of, 95
  cooked with butter, 95
    and cream, 95
  cooked with ham and onion (alla Borghese) , 96
  French style, 96
  frozen, use of, 94
  in their pods, 96
  pudding, 97
  soup, 154
Peperoni, 32–36
  farciti, 34–35
  fritti, 36
  alla Spagnuola, 33
Peppers, 32–36
  deep-fried, with tomato sauce, 36

Ravioli (*continued*)
home-made, with chicken filling, 145
Ribbon noodles (*see also* Fettucini; Tagliatelle) :
with cheese and cream, 139
with hare sauce, 144
timbale, 143
with tomatoes, garlic, and sausages (Romagna style) , 147
Rice, 132–137
how to cook, 132
leftover cooked, croquettes of, 137
pilaf, 132, 133, 136
risottos, 132 (*see also* Risottos)
Ristori (with sausage and cabbage) , 133
tomato rice, 134
Riso, 132–137
crocchette di, 137
pilaf, 133
allo zafferano, 136
al pomodoro, 134
alla Ristori, 133
Risotto, 132
ai funghi secchi (with dried mushrooms) , 134
ai gamberi (with prawns) , 135
alla Milanese (Milanese style) , 137
alla Poggio Gherardo (with marsala and chicken livers) , 136

Romaine (Cos) lettuce, dressing for, 84
Russian mixed salad, 131

Saffron pilaf, 136
Salads:
beet, 18
Cardinal (beets, radishes, cucumber, and eggs) , 129
celeriac remoulade, 47
chicken vegetable, 131
chicory, 51
cucumber, 59
eggplant and tomato, 67
fennel, 68
Italian (potatoes, carrots, and leeks) , 130
of lettuce, dressings for, 84–85
Macedonian (beans and peas) , 130
mixed, 129–131
mushroom, 90
potato:
with egg and tuna, 110
with wine and anchovies, 109
Russian (asparagus, beans, peas, carrots, anchovies, and prawns) , 131
tomato, 124
Sauces:
Beurre Fondu, 10
cheese, 43
Hollandaise, 2
lemon mayonnaise, 16
Mornay, 49

Janet Ross

For a note on Janet Ross, see the Foreword by
Sir Harry Luke.

Michael Waterfield

Michael Waterfield is a cook of renown and a
restaurateur. He is the owner of the Wife of Bath
Restaurant at Wye, in Kent, England, where
almost all the dishes in this book have been
served.